Rod Harrison's
Braid & Gelspun SUPERLINES

Rod Harrison's
Braid & Gelspun
SUPERLINES

Illustrations by
Trevor Hawkins

First published in 2011
by Australian Fishing Network
PO Box 544, Croydon, VIC 3136
Telephone: +61 3 9729 8788
Facsimile: +61 3 9729 7833
Email: sales@afn.com.au
Website: www.afn.com.au

USA Bookseller: Cardinal Publishers Group
7301 Georgetown Road, Suite 118 Indianapolis, IN 46268
Voice: (317) 879 0871 Facsimile: (317) 879 0872
Toll Free: (800) 296 0281
Website: www.cardinalpub.com

AUS: ISBN 9781 8651 3201 3
USA: ISBN 9781 8651 3207 5

Printed in China

FOREWORD

If you are using the modern braided lines (gel spun polyethylene—also called GsP around the world) with your light tackle you need this book. In the 1950s the acceptance of monofilament revolutionized the way people fish with spinning, fly and revolving reels. *Braided lines are offering just as much impact on how we fish today.* We need different reels, rods and an understanding of what is commonly called gel spun lines. There are many kinds of gel spun lines and it is important you know what type you need for your fishing and maybe more important what types you should not use.

No one understands it better than Australian, Rod Harrison, who everyone calls Harro. Harro is an iconic pioneer angler who has caught everything from small estuary species to billfish around the world.

I have met many great anglers; one of the best is Harro. He is built like a bank vault with a square body, powerful legs, a torso that says strength and forearms the size of my thighs. He is probably the most respected fishing writer in Australia. He is one the most interesting characters I have ever met. Australia is known as the land of "interesting characters" and from my experience there I would rate Harro as near the top of the heap.

We were in remote New Guinea on the Kulu River to make a film catching the strongest fish I ever encountered, the Niugini black bass. It's a fanged fish from hell that lies in ambush under sunken trees in the jungle then darts out grabs its prey and immediately retreats among the downed branches. Someone asked "how big do they get?" I answered "I don't know we could never land the bigger ones."

We found a sunken tree and with cameras rolling the 20 foot heavy fiberglass Yamaha workboat eased into position. I cast a large Deceiver fly close the branches and a big, green "thing" darted out grabbed the fly and disappeared. Even today few have caught this surly, powerful fish on fly. So Harro was anxious to film the catch.

Placing his one huge arm and hand on the left stern of the boat he grabbed a stout limb and attempted to lift the tree. The tree never moved but one of us suddenly noticed he was pushing the heavy workboat stern underwater. We yelled to stop. That fish got away but we remained in a dry boat

There are two names concerning GsP lines foreign to monofilament lines users that need to be understood (carrier and pik) and Harro explains this thoroughly. At this writing the world supply of raw GsP yarn come from limited sources. Makers are DSM in the Netherlands and their American plant, the Honeywell Corporation and Nippon Dyneema. As far as names go Honeywell still make Spectra, the rest make Dyneema. The GsP yarns come in a number of diameters (deniers), some incredible small. The companies selling fishing line purchase the raw GsP and make braided lines for customers. Harro explains why various companies' braiding techniques result in braided lines greatly different in performance and why you might want avoid or buy a specific product.

He points out that unlike monofilament, the maximum strength of knots with gel spun is not more than 70 percent. Many monofilament knots, including the famed Bimini Twist are not recommended. He does list a very few knots that will work—some new to almost anyone. This chapter on knots is one of the best I've read.

Fishermen may need different reels and rods and even lures for their fishing and this is thoroughly covered. One of the best chapters is how to fight a large variety of fish with all three types of tackle. This book gives the angler necessary knowledge of gel spun lines and how they are made and differ. It covers everything—reels, casting, selecting the right tackle, properly installing braided lines, fighting and finally landing the fish.

Lefty Kreh

"Nothing makes a fish grow more
than almost being caught"

CONTENTS

INTRODUCTION

You'd think that a long-winded technical title like gel spun polyethylene would have been made simpler by trade names made up of seven letters. Spectra and Dyneema roll off the tongue okay and mean the same stuff. However a decision, typically American, to establish a dual identity was to sew seeds of confusion that still flourish more than a decade later. Fortunately, when countries are separated by the same oceans that join fishermen the message gets through in the fullness of time.

The mountain of myth and misinformation still surrounding Spectra/Dyneema lines can be traced back to a rushed release. An angling populace, comfortable with monofilaments that had reached a developmental peak, suddenly found themselves confronted by superlines that promised the World—and a first batch didn't deliver. The assumption was a filament of Einstein complexity would be instantly grasped in Ozarks bass backwoods or the barra belt of Australia's deep north. As with a lot of new technology, not everyone knew how to take full advantage of advances offered and accommodate growing pains.

The media hasn't exactly been a source of enlightenment. Magazine superline features tend to be shallow treatments not containing technical insight beyond that claimed on packaging coming with the line. Conveniently, advertising for this brand or that isn't too far away. American magazines have done a better job than their Australian counterparts in the way information is presented but dwell on a 'Spectra won't bite' theme.

Then there's the World Wide Web. Messages in bottles set adrift on the currents of cyberspace reach many shores. But with lines crossed at the top, it was inevitable that pieces of the message would be lost. The net is awash with a million opinions, not all of them right.

So that we're all on the same page, my drafts take a couple of linguistic liberties. Dyneema/Spectra lines are collectively referred to as superlines, gel spuns, GsP and braids—the latter usage going with the assumption that by now fisherfolk are conversant with the fact that manufacturing processes other than braiding are employed. Fisho

IGFA Hall of Famer Jack Erskine preparing baits for a day of bluewater light tackle fishing. Jack's meticulous preparation has been a major factor behind his outstanding success in fresh and salt waters.

Don McPherson 1937-2006

lingo has a way of cutting through the excesses of formal English and now that Spectra and Dyneema are both made in America, the confusion should ease as generic references prevail. I hope my verbal shortcuts straighten out some curves in the road.

This book is about sorting fact from the fiction that has attached itself to this miracle fibre. It is also about tapping into a vast potential on all kinds of water. Rather than stall on stuff we already know, the extraordinary sensitivity of gel spun lines and the unprecedented situation awareness they provide, the intent is to take readers into new territory with a much more proactive approach to rigs, presentations and fights. Once understood and applied, the unique characteristics of this Space Age fibre will boost performance levels and open up new horizons, gurgling crystal clear trout streams to ocean depths where everything has big eyes.

The advent of gel spuns has intensified the knots and rigs debate. There will always be divisions, though I'm hoping that by dealing in facts and not just opinion we get to the bottom of those gnarly

issues. My research and testing would have been inconclusive were it not for access to research data and state of the art test equipment at the Brisbane plant of the Australian Monofil Company. I'm indebted to CEO Stewart McPherson for casting an eye over my drafts and giving a thumbs up to the technical veracity.

No one knew more about fishing lines than Don McPherson. And not just from chemical and molecular perspectives, but those that go with being attached to some of the world's great line burners. Don always took time to answer my questions, no matter how dumb. It isn't until someone close is gone that the influence they've had on your life sinks in. This book is for him as much as it is for me.

There have been American, European and Australian friends who've shared thoughts, boats and fishing spots—building blocks for this book, you can be sure. My words probably fail to convey the dash of colour that goes with their presence. I hope I'm excused, I'd hate to sound like a serial namedropper. Books with a technology base can be boring but I hope this one is an exception and is able to hold down a spot in the bookshelves of informed fisherfolk.

Words do not seem enough to thank Lefty Kreh for his generous foreword. Nor would money ever buy the credibility his lines carry. No one has opened as many doors. And not just for me.

A special thanks to Rick Pope, David Lee and George Smith for comments and feedback from an American perspective. Across the wide Pacific things still…grin… can be lost in translation. Highly respected and worldly Netherlands fishing writer Jeroen Schoondergang has been an invaluable assistance in establishing a contact with DSM, and the supply of interesting and creative shots of European sportfish. Through my 40 year friendship with Jack Erskine much priceless insight has been gained into the physics and mechanics of fishing tackle. Jack is a giant in the field, recently inducted into the IGFA Hall of Fame. Jack has always been able to fight above his weight with flawless rigging and black belt rodwork. To my ornery cobber of many years, Max Garth—who knows as much as anyone about gel spun polyethylene—thanks mate, your input is as valued as your friendship.

Thanks also to Shane Mensforth, Nicola Zingarelli, Steve Cooper, Paul Dolan, Peter Morse, Dave Downie, Damon Olsen of Nomad Charters, Tim Bailey, Johnny Mitchell, young gun Carl Jocumsen, and bluewater supremo Dean Butler for photography so generously given.

Lines produced from GsP fibres represent the biggest technological advance in fishing tackle since graphite rods. Gel spuns increase and enhance the connection between angler and fish like never before. A missing link finally found.

Sweet Home Awoonga,
July '11

TFO president Rick Pope out product testing.

Chapter ONE

THE ORIGIN OF LINE

Silkworms to space age fibres, cat gut to gel spuns, the evolution of fishing lines parallels a fair chunk of man's ascent from cave man to space man. In a timeless pursuit, our hunter and gatherer ancestors fished because they had to, and used what little they had. We fish because we're able, and while facing an equation of diminishing returns in many places, more lines in the water placing temptation in the way of less fish, we're in it for the fun. Were it not for technology, that refining of links between us and fish, slack lines would be the order of the day.

The Pharaohs fished lines made from animal sinew to battle Nile perch. Hooks were one of the great inventions of the Bronze Age. In an Orient that the Mediterranean World didn't know existed, silkworms were used to produce fishing lines. The first reels of antiquity were Chinese, the invention of some peaceful Confucian character. The man himself is quoted on wise men taking delight in water. During that epoch China stumbled upon gunpowder and rocketry, but—sobering thought—needed western technology and the arrival of the 21st Century to follow through.

The ancient Polynesians navigated by the stars a thousand years before the discovery of their islands by Cook. They used elbow grease and lines plaited from palm frond to subdue ahi, the fish we know as yellowfin tuna; smokers in fishspeak. The burning irony

Performance gains aside, the sheer physical weight of reels that would carry sufficient mono and hefty fibreglass blanks were burdens in themselves.

The initial mass uptake of gel spuns in English speaking countries was amongst anglers primarily fishing freshwaters but soon spread to salt.

is inescapable; ahi is also the Polynesian word for fire, slowing down a tearaway hundred pounder would be like grabbing a live welding rod.

Machine woven lines were amongst the cargo brought on by the industrial revolution. The first generations were made from flax. Fibres from the flax plant had been used in fabric and cordage since biblical times and endure today.

Linen became a refined form, produced from finer fibres, though the term these days has become broadly generic to include cloths made from artificial fibres. Linen lines have a place in the literature of fly fishing. The writers of that era when fly fishing per se meant trout, made mention of busying themselves with washing, drying and re-waxing their lines whilst anticipating the season to come. Oceanic gamefishers' offsiders performed similar maintenance. One Australian identity had a case of the smarts in adapting a bicycle with a tyre removed from the rear wheel as a line winder. That snippet passed on by the late Peter Goadby, author and encyclopaedia on things fishing. Regular maintenance warded off the rot to which linen lines were susceptible.

A peak refinement in multi-strand linen lines occurred during the times of Zane Grey. A grading system for the lines used to subdue billfish, sharks and tuna. A reference system evolved, based on the number of individual strands comprising the line. The going rate was about three pounds per thread. The Tuna Club of Avalon, on Santa Catalina Island off LAX, devised a line class system that was adopted by The International Game Fish Association when it formed in later years. These days, six thread is the IGFA #20 class, nine thread the #30 class, and so on. Avalon's membership criterion was the capture of a hundred pound blue fin tuna, on 24 thread line. To this day, the specification is for the capture to be made on either a linen or Dacron line. The Bay of Islands Swordfish Club, a Zane Grey legacy tucked away in Russell on the NZ North Island, followed suit in broadly following the Avalon template. To wander off-topic, being in the saddle with Larry McMurtry and Louis L'Amour is an easier ride.

A mass produced variety of cordage saw extensive use through the first half of the 20th Century. Produced by line makers in America, Australia and Europe, Cuttyhunk cord was dyed a distinctive dark green and became an enduring entity in both commercial and recreational sectors.

In pre-downrigger times, metallic lines saw usage as trolling equipment in North America's Great Lakes, the North Sea and New Zealand where the broad technique was, and still is, called harling. During encounters with three pound rainbow trout there's barely a wiggle to be felt—not a surprising outcome when the line weighs more than the fish. Coated lead core types provided a less weighty and more flexible intermediary that also lost out the precision that downriggers can position lures in the water column.

Synthetics take over

Following on from the industrial revolution, emerging technologies based not on contraptions but chemistry began to change the face of fishing. During the 1930s, an industrial chemist named Carothers, then in the employ of DuPont de Nemours & Co., began experiments involving carbon and other natural elements. The resulting compounds underwent refinements, and as war clouds gathered, a new flexible filament with a superior strength to diameter ratio was born.

THE BIG BANG

The inventing is ingenious, the symbolism inescapable. Combining atoms, heat, expansion and cooling, DSM went about creating its own big bang.

The process is called gel spinning and has a base material known in the petrochemical industry as ultra high modulus weight polyethylene and more often the acronym UHMWPE. It is a white semi-translucent thermoplastic by-product of ethylene with a multitude of everyday uses including artificial hips and kitchen cutting boards.

Industrial chemists at DSM discovered that when a highly refined form of UHMWPE was treated with a solvent and heated to a precise temperature, the mix became a gel that could be force fed through a spinneret by an extruder to produce a filament finer and stronger than anything extant.

A controlled ambient air temperature then cools the filament, which is then fed into a water bath for further cooling and to remove solvent traces. An end result is a fibre possessing extremely high molecular orientation, those invisible load bearing links that make some filaments stronger and tougher than others.

Down in the micro universe, stage one sees an alteration of the molecular structure of the polyethylene as it becomes suspended in a gel state. Molecules that normally form in galaxy-like clusters become disentangled and remain in that state. Then, as the filaments are drawn through an aperture so small that it has to be drilled by a space age laser, a molecular re-orientation takes place. Individual molecules link chain-like rather than the higgledy-piggledy entanglements of other extruded fibres. The degrees of stretching taking place between heating and cooling further aligns the molecules and produces deniers that are finer still.

Nylon saw much usage during World War II, though none with the same notoriety as the stockings in the hands of American military personnel—in England and Australia, and in for a good time. Diamonds weren't always a girl's best friend. In post-war years, nylon lines replaced 'cat gut' in industrialised nations.

Amongst the technology spoils discovered in Germany at war's end was a product to be named Perlon. This filament was more technically advanced than nylon and was actually the first copolymer. Nylon makers in America, Australia and the U.K. were quick to incorporate the improvements Perlon offered into their products. Despite the industrial plundering, the Bayer Company rose phoenix-like from Leverkusen, in a devastated Ruhr, to become one of the world's major monofilament makers.

Monofilaments are produced through an extrusion process. The hot mix exits the extrusion machine toothpaste-like. Cooling takes place as the newly brewed line is stretched on rollers, passing through a series of pre-set apertures. Besides achieving the desired diameter, this process aligns chain links in the molecular structure. The premium lines that have higher than standard gauge tensile strength to thickness ratio are given additional time on the rollers and are priced accordingly.

In striking a balance between hardness and handling—that constant line maker's equation—the chemical mix and process temperatures and times become a balancing act. Compromise is a narrow window. Too much of one thing and something else suffers.

Significantly, some first generation monofilaments, known in the business as Type 6 nylons still soldier on.

Copolymers are a more advanced genre of monofilament that possesses a duopoly of character. Rather than a single consistency all the way through, copolymers offer a hardened exterior with a softer core. The former quality comes from a surface annealing process. The overall pliability of copolymers has resulted in enhanced handling qualities. The angling community has given the copolymer 'hard/soft' marriage a thumbs up.

A second coming

Multi-filament lines had their second coming when they went from natural fibre to polyester, a nylon by-product. Braided polyester fibres became known through the fishing world as Dacron. A major technical advantage the new synthetic had over natural fibre lay in being imperviousness to the breakdown in tensile strength that occurred with prolonged and untreated immersion along with the ultra-violet radiation that goes with exposure to sunlight.

The discovery that Dacron possessed a 10 per cent elongation under load while retaining some 90 per cent knot strength found immediate favour with the game fish community. Ever since, those qualities, along with bigger line loads with a longer spool life, have endeared Dacron amongst the IGFA line class game fishers criss-crossing the world's oceans.

Polyethylene terephthalate, as Dacron is more formally known, was to be an answer to prayers for fly fishers. Those folk were desperate for a durable low stretch backing. The consequences of monofilament are that when recovered under pressure and thus in a stretched condition, a deal of compression occurs as the line tries to relax. This pressure compounds with each wrap. Lightweight fly reels, perforated to save weight, often end up with distorted frames and warped spools. Dacron has been much kinder. Cortland, one of the oldest names in the fly fishing business, took a further step with finer denier polyester yarn. Micron offers a 25 per cent decrease in diameter for the same tensile strength.

Dacron went on to enjoy considerable popularity in other angling arenas. During the 1950s and 1960s, Dacron and braided nylon lines became in vogue with baitcast reel users and beach fishermen. The Penn Squidder was a reel of renown for the surf. Line makers like Gudebrod produced multi-filament 'squidding' lines. Squidding became a euphemism for the surf casting culture that developed in post war decades along America's Atlantic seaboard. The metal jig being hucked out into the breakers were called tin squids.

Squidding tackle gained a bit of a toehold on places like Coila Beach, south of Sydney but was overwhelmed by a combination of Alvey sidecast reels and Platypus nylon lines, products that still dominate Australia's beaches.

Mono makers have been able to engineer copolymers for a 12 per cent stretch, which is getting close to the 8 per cent of the best 8 carrier / 8 pik braids!

Braiding companies operate on a 24/7 basis and monitor production lines to keep machines fully loaded.

As the chemicals industry hit high gear, two new synthetic fibres were given a run as fishing line. Extruded polyethylene, a thermoplastic, proved inferior to existing copolymers. Higher hopes were held for a condensation synthetic christened poly paraphenylene terephthalamide, the discovery of Stephanie Kwolek, an industrial chemist on the DuPont payroll. Kevlar fibres as the product, thankfully, was called, were thinner and stronger than existing filaments, but more brittle. As fishing line, Kevlar proved an expensive flop. It is very susceptible to UV degradation and soaks up water at a fast rate. Structurally, the biggest defect of Kevlar is that its strength in compression is only about 10 per cent of that under tension. This translates into unacceptable knot strengths.

When fluorocarbon came along, anglers were asked to put blind faith in a refractive index between that of clear mono and spring water. The marketing spin doctors declared the stuff therefore invisible to fish. Believers and sceptics are still arguing.

Braids ideally complement today's faster and more responsive graqphite composite rods

PATENTS

After encapsulating the process in a watertight world patent, DSM licensed the gel spinning process to the US, Japan and now China. Breaches, real and alleged, have been the subject of vigorous litigation. Some idea of the complexities involved might be gathered by a browse through a similar fishing line patent out there in the public domain.

United States Patent 6148597 - Manufacture of polyolefin fishing line

Fishing lines are made by a process that includes the step of exposing an opaque yarn made from ultrahigh molecular weight, gel spun polyolefin filaments to a temperature within the melting point range of the filaments for a time sufficient to at least partially fuse the contact surfaces of adjacent filaments. For ultrahigh molecular weight, gel spun polyethylene, this temperature is preferably within the range from about 150°–157° C. The surface fusion between and among filaments imparts desirable handling characteristics to the ultrahigh molecular weight, gel spun polyolefin yarns and fishing lines that are similar to those of a conventional monofilaments. Preferably, the temperature, residence time, and stretching ratio at the selected temperature are chosen to provide a fishing line exhibiting a tensile modulus within the range from about 230 g/d to about 780 g/d with a tenacity of at least 15 g/d.

There is absolutely no doubt that wary fish will take a higher percentage of flies that are delivered on leaders with a lighter bite tippet or terminal end. The issue there, imho, isn't whether the leader be nylon, copolymer or fluorocarbon, but that it's thinner.

Double Dutch

In the fading years of the last millennium, DSM High Performance Fibers, based in The Netherlands industrial centre of Heerlen unveiled Dyneema, a microfine gel spun polyethylene fibre possessing 16 times the tensile strength of steel and which could be produced in runs of unprecedented length. To quote DSM, a single GsP fibre has a 'parallel orientation greater than 95% and a high level of crystalinity, up to 85%.'

Translated to normalspeak, those figures provide a strength to diametre ratio that far outstrips any filament technology has so far, or is likely to, deliver.

DSM wisely tied up the loose ends before going public. The trade name of Dyneema was duly accorded, the manufacturing process given the protection of a

watertight patent and a triumvirate with affiliates in America and Japan was created to control world supply.

A manufacture agreement DSM entered into with the Toyobo Textile Company matured into a joint venture, Nippon Dyneema. A similar manufacturing agreement was entered into with Allied Signal, an American security equipment maker. For reasons that ever since have been a matter of some confusion amongst the global angler community, Allied Signal came up with the trade name of Spectra and oversaw the making of the world's first designated GsP line, given the catchy

The quicker fights braids permit limit opportunities for fish stealing predators attracted by a prolonged struggle.

name of Spiderwire. Allied Signal trod on DSM's toes by aggressive marketing in Europe, turf DSM considered theirs. In reprisal, DSM withheld technology, and for a time Spectra lagged technically behind Dyneema. That slack has since been taken up by the acquisition of Allied Signal by the Honeywell Corporation. In a profitable venture DSM opened a Dyneema production plant in Greenboro, North Carolina. The US defence department spends $3 billion annually on body armour. It's probable that figure will increase given continued conflicts around the globe, urban terrorism and more cops in the line of fire.

The fishing proliferation of Spectra/Dyneema places multi-filament lines in a new spotlight. In what's been a natural progression, some makers have produced blends where other fibres are mixed with GsP fibres. Another process sees a GsP core given a copolymer coating—pretty much the same way it's done in fly lines production. Some disadvantage lays in diameters that are getting back towards monofilament gauges. It will be interesting to see how long they stay around.

In another development that's gone nowhere, the Japanese have produced lines from another ultra fine filament known as Zylon. It has commendable tensile strength but is rapidly ravaged by ultra-violet radiation. The Yo Zuri company has put a toe in the water with a commercial batch. It didn't sell. However, the search for a UV inhibitor goes on.

Into the foreseeable future, the ongoing spread of gel spuns is assured. Shrinking world fisheries and fish that are either getting smarter or smaller are dynamics that compel the focused angler to seek out every equipment advantage. Rod materials are pretty much at a modulus dead end, and reels may have reached a developmental peak (given the emphasis on cosmetics by the big makers). The same course seems charted for gel spuns. The end of the line.

COMMERCIALISM NOT CONFLICT

The Dutch are an interesting race. Rather than make the wars that bled the empires of England, France, Spain and Portugal, the Dutch figured it was easier to make money—but not before producing mariners who should be mentioned in the same breath as Cook and Columbus. Willem Janszoon (1570–1630) was the first European to sight Australia, Dirk Hartog (1580–1621) the second to set foot.

That's not to say the Dutch are strangers to combat, medieval or modern. Australian and Dutch troops share the same base in Afghanistan. Over Bosnia, a Dutch F16 pilot downed a MIG-29 in that theatre's only encounter between fourth generation fighter jets. Those same skies claimed a hundred million dollar US Air Force stealth bomber, quite possibly to a stray ten cent rifle round. Commerce and culture rather than conflict is synonymous with Holland's 16 million. Along with giving the civilised world a political liberalism and a per capita record of sporting achievement second to none, the latest the World Cup final. And Andre Rieu.

Chapter TWO

IN THE RAW

My broad explanation of the gel spinning process poses questions. Do gel spuns have to be multi-filament lines? Yes. Can GsP be extruded as a monofilament? No, not as fishing line. Gel spun polyethylene is a stiff fibre. The fibres have a modulus of elasticity between 90 and 120, depending on denier. To give those figures some context, they lay between those applicable to the e-glass and graphite composites used for fishing rods. Such a resistance to bending imposes radius limitations. Were a single GsP fibre extruded in a gauge similar to 50 pound monofilament, it would require a spool the size of a bicycle wheel and possess the memory of an elephant that's had a bowel irrigation. In the scaled down case of fishing lines and sensible fishing usage there's no apparent lack of flexibility. However when stresses on the line approach break point, down in the micro world of individual fibres, a fatal cocktail of creep and slippage brings on a critical radius and a chain reaction.

A long yarn

Commercial quantities of GsP yarn come in a number of deniers. The term relates to a standard of measure the British originally devised to grade the fineness of silk. It has since been adapted to man made fibres but still contains the quirks of the Imperial weights and measures system. For example, one gram of a 'one' denier fibre has a length of 9000 metres. Gel spinning yields continuous runs of many thousands of metres. A few kilograms of the finest denier will reach the moon!

To measure GsP's astounding tensile strength another way, if one were to suspend a single fibre in a length long enough that it fractured by its own weight, it would be over 250 miles long.

Raw GsP yarns have denier and price parallels with wool, that enduring natural fibre of which the higher microns, a thinner fibre, is used to make Italian suits, the broader types, carpets. The relatively 'coarse' GsP yarns are used (in mega strand batches) for ropes, fishing nets, cordage, protective clothing and for reinforcement of impact-resistant composites.

The strands that go into most fishing lines can be counted on one's fingers. In the case of thermofused and coated types, and the majority of braids, one hand will be enough! Raw material costs rather than a long and happy spool life has become the key decision in the number of raw yarn strands to go into the construction of a gel spun line. Unlike the established monofilament

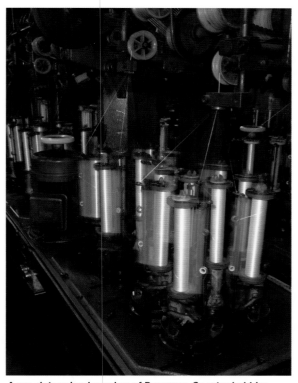

A pre-determined number of Dyneema-Spectra bobbins – according to the carrier count of the line – are mounted onto braiding machines.

market, where a higher cost for heavier line is indexed to the amount of raw material involved, the pricing of raw GsP yarn reflects a reversal of that trend. Shades of railways, there is no standardisation of denier gauges amongst makers. DSM offer SK60, SK65 and SK75 yarns, descending deniers that ascend in price by a factor of fifty percent. Similarly, Honeywell make Spectra 1000, Spectra 2000 and Spectra 2200. Nippon Dyneema produces deniers that are even finer, but not available for export.

Body armour accounts for much production. Though superior to the Kevlar in widespread use in protective vests, the jury is still out whether Spectra/Dyneema takes the pace out of a small bullet quite the same as it does a big fish.

No one's saying whether the new material will handle a direct hit from an AK-47, a weapon that's that probably killed and maimed more people than any other modern

Braiding machines are a mechanical wonder that computer technology hasn't been able to improve.

Quality control is maintained by regular and random testing of batches for tensile and knot strengths along with abrasion resistance.

firearm. To be subjective, I've fired a lot of 7.62 x 39 mm rounds at wild boars from an SKK, but have far more faith in Winchester's tried and true .30-30, which is all the better for Hornady's 160 grain Lever-lution round. However, the question may not be in the affirmative as far as newer versions of the Kalashnikov are concerned. They fire a 5.45 x 39 mm cartridge that's 1000 feet per second faster. The equation boils down to a trade off of impact kinetics for greater penetration—not the sort of thing conducive to long queues of volunteers when it comes to testing body armour.

Stretching the facts

Contrary to written and popularly held opinion, GsP does stretch. The raw fibre exhibits an elongation of 3.5 per cent before rupturing. For practical purposes this can be extended to a surprising and very handy 8 per cent through the concertina effect of a specialised braiding process that just a few line makers use.

There's an overlooked side to the stretch equation. This isn't apparent with double digit breaking strain braids, but when branded breaking strains get down into single figures, busted lines become a more frequent event. Sudden stress is the culprit; force with kinetics beyond the tensile strength of the line, applied with the speed of an Ali jab. The stretch in monofilaments acts as an inbuilt cushion able to decelerate those forces.

The absence of a built-in buffer in braids doesn't alter the fact that fishermen break more lines than do fish. But then, they're probably more aware of Murphy's Law than those of Sir Isaac Newton.

Fatigue is another matter. The stresses that go with bump and grind of hard fishing compound to form hot spots. These develop at pressure points such as the core of knots, where the line hinges at the rod tip during prolonged casting and gel spun/leader connections having high speed collisions with rod runners. Neglect there is asking for a tackle failure.

Impervious nature

Raw GsP contain other qualities of interest to anglers. The opaque whitish fibres have a specific gravity slightly less than that of water. Being molecularly watertight, they float and are impervious to chemical intrusion. This immunity is a major headache for braid makers. At best, their treatments are skin deep. Those urethane based brews are spiked with resins and colouring pigment. Despite statements that these cocktails permeate the inner core of fibres, they eventually wear and leech with time and use. Lines return to the off-white tone of the raw fibres.

Colour loss has absolutely no detrimental impact on tensile strength. A Dyneema line on one of my workhorse baitcast reels is now into its second decade and though reverting to the off-white colour of the raw yarn has caught over a ton of barramundi by now. Such can be a long and happy spool life.

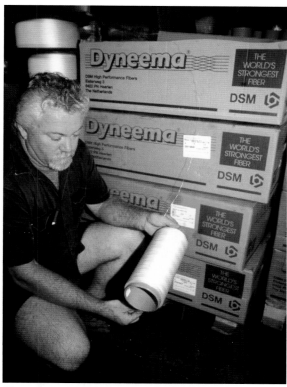

The makers of GsP raw yarns supply line makers with various deniers on spools of enormous meterage.

Colour loss is a tangible consequence when spooling up. Although there has been a vast increase in the durability of resins makers apply to GsP lines, little piles of pigmentation build up on rod guides, the level wind gates of baitcast reels and on fingers applying pinch pressure. Fisherfolk who've just forked out a hundred bucks for a spool of line may view the residue as if they've just wasted a few dollars but there's no cause

for alarm. Colour loss to any quality working line soon stabilises and becomes imperceptible. A final harp: there is absolutely no connection between fade and any loss of tensile strength, real or imagined.

Gel spuns are UV resistant. The ultra-violet radiation effect, the impact of direct sunlight that can reduce marlin gauge monofilaments to the strength of cotton, doesn't occur.

Here's the rub

The lab specs on GsP are impressive. At a microscopic level, GsP yarn forms in long molecular chains. The result is strengthened intermolecular interactions that effectively bear and transfer load to a polymer backbone. The statistic about a tensile strength, micron for micron, much superior to carbon steel creates a sense of security. Then there's that slippery nature—on paper a friction reduction dynamic that should translate into less wear and tear. Should! Unfortunately, slippage under load makes its way into the innards of the tightest knots to cause the instabilities to which this text has already alluded.

In wars with rocks, snags, weeds and hard headed fish, the biggest thing GsP has going is diameter. Put simply, thicker lines distribute wear through having more bearing surface over which to spread the gouging and shredding effect of jagged surfaces. Thinner lines result in the same wear and tear concentrated over a narrower band and therefore penetrating deeper into the line. To get all this in context, were we to be saddled with gel spuns the same diameter as the monofilaments of our previous lives, the capacity for hard knocks would be astronomical.

There are two sides to the abrasion equation. GsP lines have the welcomed capacity to 'saw' through soft matter such as weeds. An ability to endure contact with smooth objects such as drowned timber. There, quick thinking anglers manage fish that run around snags by reducing pressure by free spooling and using thumb control. Reels are re-engaged when the line is clear. That move

Amongst smooth surfaces like acquatic vegetation Spectra-Dyneema lines have admirable abrasion resistance.

Badlands. Shale and rip-rap have shown up the braids' Achilles Heel.

isn't an option in tidal waters where sticks are barnacle encrusted. As harped about already, GsP hates rough, raspy surfaces.

Is seeing believing?

Gel spun polyethylene fibre is off-white and far more opaque than transparent. When bonded into fishing lines, sales are more assured by a dash of colour.

We have no trouble seeing the solid colours of GsP lines and assume fish also can. That's abundantly clear when dealing with wary species in shallows where they have extreme visibility.

Deeper waters are different. There's a belief that oceans are sparkling clear water and fish see everything. The fact is that oceans are 'bottomless' in most cases and the background is usually very dark. The surface layer is filled with light beams moving in time with the ocean swells. This is why fish and lures with vertical bars can be visible or invisible in those grating beams. At depths below 10 metres 'red light' disappears off the colour spectrum. This is why a number of inshore demersal fish are a shade of grey down amongst reef habitat, but yanked topside on the end of a line they're variously red, crimson and pink. Pelagic species do not have a red sensor in their eye structure, but that doesn't stop the widespread and successful use of red and pink lures. They don't have a red sensor so they don't see the full spectrum of colours.

The issue is even more clouded in freshwaters. Twenty feet down in lakes that we may regard as clear and very fishable it can be pretty black. The upwards vision of predatory species can be dominated by the big back lit disc that's brought about by Snell's law of refraction. Fish within that disc probably see everything it contains.

Because gel spuns are very thin and fish are more interested in what's on the end rather than where it leads, it mightn't matter. Fish have a physical disadvantage in not having eyelids or a variable pupil. This limits the time they can spend in shallows or close to the surface in bright light.

In pressured waters, especially lakes, there's no doubt fish become conditioned. It's an open question as to the extent of their memory retention, whether milliseconds or minutes or maybe more. Long enough, you can be sure, to be suspicious of things like fake fish with strings attached.

The addition of a mono leader alleviates concerns about visibility and boosts the confidence factor. Conditions may call for a simple, clear nylon, a non-glint type, or fluorocarbon. If the latter, make sure it is a 'pure' brand.

Reserve Powers

It has become an unofficial industry standard for gel spuns to carry stated breaking strains around twice that of the unknotted tensile strength of the line to which the packaging relates. No one's saying so, especially the marketers behind so many brands, but the intent in overstated breaking strains is to factor in knots. The best knots may yield percentage breaks in the order of 70 per cent, the worst can reduce the line by 50 per cent, which isn't such a bad worst case scenario when one considers that the firepower in the lines is still pretty close to the stated breaking strain.

Trevally and other bulldogging fish highlight the vulnerability of braids around abrasive surfaces – and the need for leaders.

Below: Teeth rather than territory dictate the rigging for open water sprinters like Spanish Mackerel.

BRAIDS AIN'T BRAIDS

The term *braids* is entrenched as a generic reference to all lines produced from gel spun polyethylene fibres. There's no doubting that it rolls the easiest off the tongue, but it ignores the fact that all 'braids' aren't created equal. Today's welter of brands, the flood following the famines of yesteryear, has an 'out of the box' equality. Breaking strains and knot strengths are dependant on the amount of raw fibre in the line, not any manufacture special process or magic potion. Like car tyres, every fishing line wears with use. Indisputably, a steel belt radial outperforms and outlasts a retread, but costs more. The world of superlines has a similar tiered quality array along with tradeoffs.

Manufacturing Processes

Twisted and waxed

Cost	Handling & Performance	Durability
☆☆☆☆☆	☆☆	☆☆

Where and How Made

This type of gel spun comes from European makers. The fibres are machine twisted and passed though a wax type bath that gives the line exterior a soft clammy feel.

Advantages

Cheaper manufacture due to 'coarse' denier yarn and relatively cost effective production line. Those costs are not always passed onto the consumer.

Disadvantages

The 'sticky' texture of these lines contributes to backlashes and hinders casting distance.

Inferior wear. For a time, the handling qualities of twisted and waxed braids are almost acceptable—as if broken in—however the wax type compounds used as a sealing agent rapidly leech from the fibres thereby accelerating wear.

Handling hassles. Line management, becomes increasingly difficult as the fibres in twisted and waxed gel spuns lose support as increased use disintegrates the sealing wax.

Thermo-fused

Cost	Handling & Performance	Durability
☆☆☆☆	☆☆☆	☆☆

Where and How Made

USA and possibly under licence in Canada.

Berkley Fireline was the original thermo-fused line. It is produced by a cost effective process that sees the fibres bunched and passed through an element which heats and melts their outside surface thereby forming a finish. The process was the subject of a patent vigorously protected.

Since Berkley—and once rival line makers—have been absorbed into the Pure Fishing conglomerate, other gel spun lines, not necessarily thermo-fused types, have been included in and marketed under the Fireline brand.

Advantages

Lower cost. (Original) Fireline is still made from a less costly denier raw GsP yarn. The manufacturing process is, likewise, cost and time efficient. Those factors give Fireline advantageous price points, moreso at the ultra light tackle end of the market.

Fine diameter. A heat shrink side effect to the process provides thermo-fused lines with a finer diameter to strength ratio than what can be achieved with other manufacture methods.

Widely available. Pure Fishing is the world's largest marketer of gel spun lines. Amongst a stable of 'Firelines' the original version remains the biggest seller.

Disadvantages

Wiry texture. Thermo-fused lines have a wiry texture. This may or may not suit individual users. In broad terms however, texture and handling concerns extending from texture are probably the most commonly cited criticisms.

Rapid wear. With hard use, the outer surface of thermo-fused lines chips and flakes. Exposed thus, the fibres are subject to rapid wear and rupture. Furry sections along the surface of the line signpost a line that's running out of time.

Coated Gel Spuns

Cost	Handling & Performance	Durability
☆☆☆☆	☆☆☆	☆☆☆

Where and How Made

A gel spun genre that may well be termed 'coated' are produced under contract in North America and possibly elsewhere. Their manufacture is somewhat akin to that of fly lines—where a central fibre core received a flexible coating with a compound containing flexible plasticizers. In these instances the fibres are aligned, given integrity through a twist process then treated with a non-residual chemical bath.

Advantages

Lower costs. Consumers should benefit from the less costly gauge raw yarns employed, along with a time and cost effective process that results in a cheaper overall manufacturing process,

Improved handling. Coated braids have a degree of stiffness that has wide angler support.

Disadvantages

Thicker diameter. Coated braids have marginally thicker diameters than other braids of comparable strength. This translates into lessened reel capacities and shorter casts

Coaxial and Hybrid Braids

Cost	Handling & Performance	Durability
☆☆☆☆	☆☆☆☆	☆☆☆☆

Where and How Made

This relatively new production method, underway in North America, Japan and Europe, involves gel spun fibres spiral wrapped around a central core fibre. In some cases, the construction is eight carrier—all one and the same—seven strands, woven around a central longitudinal strand.

Hybrid braids are produced by substituting one or more stands (usually the central) with materials such as Dacron. Kevlar and polypropylene.

Advantages

Low retail costs. A reflection in a fast production process, varied carrier counts and the substitution of a less expensive fibre in the case of hybrids.

Improved body. The construction process offers improved body over true braids with a low carrier count. This translates into better handling qualities.

Disadvantages

Larger diameters. Hybrids and braids not produced on a 7:1 ratio can have thicker diameters than contemporaries of the same strength.

Though reel capacities and casting distances can be reduced the amounts are slight.

True Braids

Type	Cost	Handling & Performance	Durability
Four Carrier	☆☆☆	☆☆☆	☆☆☆
Five Carrier	☆☆☆	☆☆☆☆	☆☆☆☆
Eight Carrier	☆☆	☆☆☆☆☆	☆☆☆☆☆

Where and How Made

True Braids are machine produced in North America, Japan, Europe and Australia.

They are produced in banks of braiding machines which run round the clock.

All things considered, braiding is the most costly of production processes. Manufacturing costs are indexed to the pik count—the number of strands used in the construction.

The finer the denier of the raw GsP yarn, the more expensive—costs ascend by a factor of fifty percent between the type SK60, SK65 and SK70 yarns that DSM offer customers.

As the finished lines come off the braiding machines they are treated with urethane based compounds that permeate the construction providing bonding and body. Some makers pre-treat fibres prior to braiding, not that this makes any difference. Gel spun polyethylene yarn is impervious to chemical intrusion and no process pre or post manufacture increases the tensile strength of the line beyond the original sum total of the fibres.

Advantages

Some—not all—true braids offer longer spool life and less handling hassles.

The higher the carrier count, the better the braid.

Braids with an eight carrier / eight pik construction have 7%+ stretch through the concertina effect of the weave.

The more rounded format of high carrier braids lays more comfortably on reel spools and generally handles better.

Disadvantages

True braids can cost more. Increased material costs and slower manufacture tend to be reflected in asking monies.

Manufacturers of four and five carrier braids tend not to announce the fact.

Under magnification, four carrier braids have a square cross section that wears faster and has marginally inferior handling qualities. Five carrier braids are pentagonal in shape and similar wear rates and handling characteristics. Eight carrier braids are octagonal and as near to a perfectly round that technology can produce.

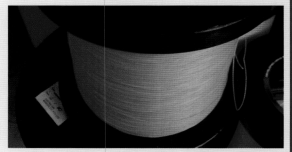

After coming off the braiding machiines Spectra-Dyneema lines have a finishing treatment applied that also contains a colouring agent.

Chapter THREE

THE FAITH SPREADS – PERSONAL REFLECTIONS

The first converts responded to messages in the sky. Fishermen were amongst folk gazing upwards from a Japanese countryside. Some wondered how paper dragons the size of a subway tunnel could soar up there amongst Cherubim and Seraphim while still having an umbilical to Mother Earth. What sort of line could be so thin, yet that strong?

Japan was the right place for Dyneema to get a kick-start into fishing. The motive and means were both in abundant supply, the latter in the form of surplus braiding machines scattered through a thousand backyards. Neighbourhood manufacturing networks had been set up as dispersal measures in desperate attempts to reduce the impact of bombing in the latter stages of the war.

In Japan's reconstruction, fishing technologies went from trained cormorants to fleets able to strip mine oceans. But the Americanising that goes with golf, baseball and sportfishing didn't totally erase a barbaric streak. A whaling programme, carried on under the shameful guise of 'scientific research' sees meat openly sold in fish markets and promoted to schoolchildren. The cetacean hit list includes the humpbacks that migrate and cavort—to the delight of thousands—their way north along the American and Australian coasts. The harpoons being used in Antarctic killing grounds— away from the world's eyes—are attached with Dyneema ropes that'd hold Godzilla. Japan's traditional fishing roots can be traced back to the lines and hooks of antiquity. There is no cultural connection with explosive devices that only came along after they lost Moby Dick.

One only has to visit the Tokyo's Tsukiji Market to figure on being in a fish mad country. A serve of tuna belly strip that'll leave you hungry costs over a hundred bucks. Sportfishing has appeal having the wherewithal on the socio-economic ladder. A thousands cadre of Japanese anglers travel to fishier waters—Alaska, Australia, New Zealand and Christmas Island. Their feedback is reflected in the depth and sophistication of arsenals that are a major cultural shock for any tackle rat.

Australian Carl Jocumsen with a largemouth bass taken in Lake Fork, Texas. Largemouth bassers are amongst the world's biggest user group for gel spun lines.

Australia is a popular destination for Japanese anglers seeking new species. This one has just caught a nice Murray cod

When Daiwa purchased British reel maker Whyte-Hall in the early 1960s, the writing was on the wall. The design and marketing people had more in mind than copycat versions with which to take on a world complacent with brands like Mitchell, ABU, Shakespeare and Zebco. A long forgotten brand, Dickson, produced some of the first Japanese made sportfishing lures. They included bootlegged versions of the Heddon Sonic and ABU Sonnette. Those crude copies bear little resemblance to today's counterfeit fish and exquisite finishes.

Following the DSM/Toyobo agreement, the ready supply of homemade Dyneema braid yarn saw Japanese sportfishers steal a march. Takahiro Omori, a most recognised face in his homeland, was a high school dropout who went fishing against parental wishes. Omori was ready by 2004, so off he went to Charlotte, North Carolina and the Bassmaster Classic. While other competitors soldiered on with monofilament, Omori was spooled up with Dyneema. His win was a public relations triumph for his sponsor, Daiwa.

Backing up a bit, California charter skipper Russ Izor was probably the first westerner to see the light. Convinced of the performance advantages of lines being used by Japanese clients, he pitched the notion to American fishing industry interests. The initial response

Floris van den Berg with a nice Zander. Dyneema lines are behind a finesse fishery that's evolved in The Netherlands.

was lukewarm; fishermen wouldn't pay that much for line. They were; IzorLine developed a cult following amongst the offshore community. But it wasn't to be all smooth sailing. Under heavy load, gel spun was deemed guilty of sins ranging from severing the mono lines of other anglers at the rail, sawing through anchor ropes, grooving rod guides and slicing any careless digit. It was banned from a number of boats. IzorLine soldiers on; these days a stable comprising a number of mono and multi-filament lines with a strong west coast support base.

Word via the fisho grapevine spread to motivated insiders who began sourcing kite string via Japanese backdoors. To take some sidetracks, I'd have never been on the Spectra/Dyneema ground floor were it not for Ed Rice, president of International Sportsmen's Expositions. ISE staged fishing and hunting shows that drew record attendances.

A sizeable bloke, Ed's generosity was just as big. After signing on to do presentations in Australia on his show circuit, Ed shouted me a long range trip out of San Diego, flyfishing for striped marlin. Between shows, stays at his house up in Washington State were highlighted by slack jawed ogling and touching in his den. I'd never seen so many Charlton reels nor such a hunting gun collection. A red Ferrari sat in the garage.

Another treat was a fishing trip on the mighty Columbia River, which gives its name to the clothing company in Portland, just across the river from the Rice ranchero. Ed Eiman had laid-back people skills and eyes just as sharp as the bald eagles gliding along the river valley. His guiding credentials included world record walleye from the Columbia mother lode. There were also sturgeon the length of a skiff. They bite on green meat that needed to be carted in a nose proof bucket.

Working with the ease of a cowboy rolling a smoke with one hand, Ed rigged a casting rod with a white bucktail jig—worldwide, still the most successful single all-round lure. I made a comment to that effect while casting along a seam made by a meeting of still and moving waters. Ed had already explained that fish hung along those edges. I thought it would be a bit smart-arse of me to mention that was stuff I already knew. I was more interested in the line. Every contact the jig made had an identifiable feel. And when a hit happened— and mind you, walleyes aren't noted for causing heart seizures when they strike—it was a jolt, not a tap. I didn't know what the hell it was. Some sort of albino sensitised Dacron? I had to ask.

If you could tap into the pipeline, 'kite line' went for a buck a yard via jobber supply chains with links to Japan. The money was there; in a dark age of stretchy monofilaments—where one had to feel the way like a blind man on a honeymoon, striking at every possibility—Dyneema lines not only heightened contacts but carried a message that defined their composition, animal, vegetable or mineral.

The long range flyfishing trip was aboard the Royal Star, a comfortable 90 footer with a highly experienced skipper and crew. The angler complement included twenty something tackle industry people, fly fishing luminaries and lodge owners. Ray Beadle and his mate Trey Combs were the masters of ceremony. Beadle had been to Australia with bonzer blokes now gone, Sage marketing manager Les Eichorn and Fishing International's Frank Bertaina. At Cape Bowling Green with skippers Bob Jones and Frank Thompson, Beadle eclipsed Billy Pate's world records for fly caught black marlin.

Running a rotational system, Beadle teased while Combs coached those new to the experience. A better man in their

The Pearl Perch is just one of many deep sea fish braids have made more accessible.

Braids have opened up a new dimension on Snapper.
Australia and New Zealand's most popular offshore species
is called the Squirrelfish elsewhere in the world.

corner they couldn't have. Combs, author of Bluewater Flyfishing—an authority in the field, you can be sure—was a big league veteran. The queue contained full rods and half rods. The 'halves' had a shot every second rotation. Mine was stuffed up going for an injudicious head-on hookup. That blood rush turned out the lesser of two big lessons. On my next shot I waited for the fish to turn before setting the hook.

Flat seas saw a speed up in the rotation. Once hooked up and the fish settled, the angler could elect to finish the fight from one of the Royal Star ducks. An inflatable isn't the best platform from which to conduct a fight. You lose something when pressure you apply draws the boat to the fish rather than the other way around. I was happy to pop a couple of fish at my rod tip rather than see them gaffed. Crewmen stuck and sold everything; some sort of fish market bonus arrangement at trips' end. Even more disturbingly irresponsible was the way galley garbage was bundled into a big plastic bag and hoiked overboard.

A spool of Spiderwire I'd been given at an American fishing show proved to be another lesson in wait. I'd been having troubles with my main workhorse reel.

A pre-production #5 Abel kindly passed on by Steve Abel for a trial was grabbing. The spool shoulders had been machined too thin. When loaded and under drag, the spool was spreading a thou' or so, jamming against a frame that also had cigarette paper tolerances. The problem went away when the backing was removed but re-occurred when the 400 yards of #30 micron was re-spooled. It was left that way to quickly make the point when the reel caught up with Steve Abel. He dealt with the hiccup cordially, decisively and professionally.

I may have made a wrong decision not to transfer the Abel backing. My backup was the biggest of a set of Lamson reels that became part of my caboodle when Sage acquired the brand. To be the first non-American on the Sage Advisory Staff carried some prestige then, gear and a quarterly cheque in American dollars. The appointment caused some angst back in Australia, me not being in the trout swim nor a tournament caster.

Whenever the forward scanning sonar indicated pods of gamefish, crewmen drew them to the boat with scoops of live-bait. The effect was dramatic, fast-tracking the rotation. And whenever a school of wahoo, yellowfin or black skipjack zeroed in on the live baits, it was every man for himself. I didn't want to be caught messing with reels when the action happened.

The Lamson easily accommodated the 200+ yards of Dacron borrowed from another reel I'd been using on tarpon in Central America. The Spiderwire top shot made a total backing load of over 500 yards, peace of mind one would think, when it comes to staying hooked to a fish famed for electrifying sprints and rampaging gymnastics.

On another flat afternoon I shared a duck with Trey. The crewman wasn't long in teasing up a striped marlin that was all over my fly the instant it hit the water. The hook set felt solid and the reel was unloading in a blur… then a sickening nothing. To cite the cliché that says it all, hero to zero. I'd lost the whole bloody flyline when the backing connection failed. It was a long afternoon. Minutes later, Trey hooked up on a beauty that didn't leap and which he was still fighting at sunset. We made the transition back to the Royal Star where Trey continued the fight, popping the fish within a whisker of waiting gaffs.

Reconstructing my disaster, I discovered that the loose weave first generation Spectra did not cinch down like mono or Dacron. Rather, it had the tendency to crib, thus converting the 'square' format of a safe loop to loop connection into a girth hitch that can result in the Spectra cutting through the other materials. On the balance of probabilities, the conclusion was thus. Supporting circumstances were that the joint had been highly stressed in previous encounters in the duck where (an already alluded) lack of grip in the water meant that slugfest part of the fight happened with the backing junction beyond the rod tip and not with the skinny end of the flyline safely back on the reel. The problem isn't as prevalent with tight weave braids but still needs watching.

Cairns based barramundi guide and marlin skipper Barry Cross did as much as anyone to spread the GsP gospel Downunder. A great caster and innovator, Barry was looking for some middle ground between barra and billfish. He found it along the countless coral edges and outcrops of the Great Barrier Reef. Tough neighbourhoods patrolled by trevally gangs always cruising for a bruising. The coke can sized chuggers Cross had taken to hurling were just right for picking a brawl with those finned Volkswagens.

Barry fine tuned his topwater technique into an art form. It was based on following the Fusiliers. A bit like a Rainbow Runner, schools of these blue and yellow striped fish stand out against the cobalt Coral Sea like a neon sign. Depending on wind or current direction they will mingle in the slacker leeward water, shadowed, by trevally, fins cocked and ever ready to create or capitalise on an incident.

That scenario—and the goods—were marketed brilliantly well to Japanese clients. From that beginning, a cult developed through the Pacific. The great trevally, Caranx ignobilis, found from Hawaii and Christmas Island westwards through the Pacific and Indian Oceans to Madagascar and Mozambique is now referred to by the Japanese as the Samurai of the Sea.

Japanese anglers visiting Australia aren't noted tippers. More yin and yang than yen, but some leave some pretty neat tackle with charter skippers following a successful trip. Barry Cross was spooled up with Dyneema line before anyone else in the country knew about the stuff. Japanese fishers' travel to Australia has since become focused on deep jigging for samson fish, a Seriola species that lays between amberjack and kingfish (California yellowtail), growing just as big.

North America's bass belt covers the biggest cult and consumer collective in the sportfishing world. It remains the major market for Spectra/Dyneema lines. First time around, Spectra was cited for a litany of lost fish. Of major concern was a lack of stretch—blamed for hook sets coming up short. Mind you, television had turned bass fishing into a 'gotta-have' consumer-thon—anglers dressed up like NASCAR drivers, drama queen hook sets, and quicker than Mike Iaconelli can holler 'EEhaaar', ol' bucketmouth is floundering on the deck.

Second time around the media bombardment is filtered through to the bass backwoods. The packaging on one brand assures buyers the line will not groove rod runners! On another, that it will not break at the knot. Whatever knot it is, I wish it could be shared with the sportfishing world. Darned if I can find it. For reasons I'll dissect later, a palomar knot offers the best percentage returns in GsP lines. Those figures are always less than the line's unknotted tensile strength. The only logical conclusion for a Spectra/Dyneema line not to break at the knot is some internal defect or outside intervention. As for allegations of grooved rod guides, I know that abrasive aramid compounds have been used in some multi-filament lines and my eyes might need testing, but in a thousand days on salt and fresh since the superlines advent, I've yet to see Spectra/Dyneema—or any other line—groove a quality metal or ceramic guide. Though superlines have become a spin doctor's picnic, the fortunate reality remains that the naysayer isn't an endangered species.

Respected rod maker G.Loomis, purchased by Shimano, saw opportunity in the confusion and misinformation surrounding Spectra. Their solution was to build on longer and softer blanks claimed to be more that accommodating of non-stretch lines. It was a backwards step.

Dyneema Debuts

Superlines in Australia were love at first bite. The uptake was rapid and with few recriminations. Fisherfolk, salt and fresh, spooled up in the sort of numbers that made them, per capita, the world's biggest user. Their overwhelming verdict is that the purgatory of learning to master gel spuns is worth a Promised Land of performance and awareness. The Platypus Line Company under Don McPherson accelerated the uptake and was producing superior gel spun lines long before the local market became swamped with imports.

Apropos, and to take a detour through Europe, I'd arranged to meet Don at a mid 1990s European Fishing Tackle Exhibition in Amsterdam. He was in The Netherlands doing business with DSM. I was there on

An Icelandic lass with a nice pair of Ling taken while pirking with braided lines.

behalf of Sage, working from the booth of their German distributor. The House of Hardy was opposite, across the casting pool. The casting pool was only six inches deep but I was out of my depth. Suited English gentlemen seemingly able to false cast a full line had me covered.

The actions of the European fly rods were slow, ten years behind what the Americans were making. Their casting methodology went back even further, that rigid hickory-dickory-dock and flourishing double hauls that ignore human bio-mechanics and energy inputs. But you could see awakening interest in faster tapers and the higher line speeds. My side arm style, aka Lefty, was a bit of a novelty amongst the Hardy Boys. Their dissertations on what they regard as 'push' casting—as against 'pull'—bamboozled, but we were in the right place for some double Dutch. Ain't it funny the way the longest casts are made in front of audiences and not to fish. And how so many who're preoccupied with distances seem in denial about 80 per cent of their best efforts being achievable with some whose hands move inches instead of yards? That's a lot of extra joint wear and tear over a lifetime of fishing.

The demountable casting pools used at fishing shows have to be sized to suit the venue and need to include space enough to accommodate long backcasts. In fitting in with the requirements of the staging organisation, it is not unusual for fly rod exhibitors to cut back hundred foot flylines to eighty something. This can contain a hidden bonus. Some fly line brands may be recognised,

along with the assumption they are full length. The distance compression that goes with an indoors perspective did the rest.

In contrast to situations in America and Australia where word about gel spuns quickly filtered down to the fishing grass roots, Dyneema had a low key EFTEX debut. European fishing line exhibitors then reflected a past rather than looking to the future. My visit uncovered monofilaments visible and as varied as sights along Amsterdam's sleaze district, and Dyneema lines that were harder to find than a church amongst those voyeur boulevards. Apart from some mild interest on the part of travelled fly fishers who'd experienced their backing being peeled, there was scant suggestion of any other fishing suitability. Things have changed since.

A drink with Gary Storm was enlightening. The discussion had initially been about lures, specifically Magnum Hot 'n' Tot, a killer lure in Australia no longer available. The talk was about it being no longer made, I'd get things straight from the horse's mouth. It was true, but matters were out of his hands. He'd sold Storm Lures to Rapala. The talk then drifted onto lines. A largemouth bass fishery in Spain followed American trends. Some future promise for superlines lay there. Salmon fisheries scattered through Iceland, Ireland,

Sunset on Lake Nasser

Scotland, Norway and more recently Russia's Kola Peninsula were stepped in tradition that wasn't likely to change. One needed to be royalty or on a pretty good payroll to fish those places. Elsewhere through Scandinavia and Europe the freshwater fishery comprised of smallish trout, pike, perch (redfin), carp, and zander, a walleye look-alike. An offshore pirk—metal lures we call jigs—targeting North Sea cod was an obvious growth area. All in all, the conversion rate was set to lag behind that taking place elsewhere.

To reconnect with GsP, the material has been used as a core material by adventurous flyline makers. The marriage hasn't worked due to a stretch and flex incompatibility with PVC coatings.

A Rocky Road

Don and I fished Egypt's Lake Nasser on the way back to Australia. The Nile perch looks a lot like a barramundi and, although growing bigger, isn't as dynamic a sportfish nor as tough on tackle. Our guides understood but two words of English but were intrigued by my barra tattoo and seemed mesmerised when I produced a flyrod and began casting. My portable fish finder drew worried looks when the alarm sounded.

Inescapable symbolism. Lates genus fish like Nile Perch and Barramundi eat flies like this Oz version of Dan Blanton's Whistler.

There they were. Nosed in tight against the sheer wall of once what had been a quarry…parked like airliners at a passenger terminal. Wherever an overhang offered enough shade a Nile perch had its head in the nook. The rest of the body exposed ostrich-like. The largest looked somewhere between eighty and a hundred pounds.

Not surprisingly, they weren't interested in the fly being jiggled in their face….little fake fish do not aggressively confront big fish. Almost reluctantly they de-materialised deeper. Casting out far as I could and working progressively deeper, I began some diagonal retrieves that roughly paralleled the rock wall.

The strike was almost gentle. A matter-of-fact tug that brought the fly to a dead stop. But in the instant or so it took for the fish to get the message, the rod bent through to the corks as my line hand applied the brakes on the remaining running line. Safely on the reel, or so I thought, the Spectra was unloading into the jade coloured lake. Then quicker than I could rationalise the thought, the rod recoiled. For a second time I'd lost the entire chain—fish, fly, leader, head and running line.

An average sized Nile Perch

Fisherfolk had to find out for themselves that rocks are the superlines' kryptonite. A single brief contact with the line paying out under load can be the kiss of death. Egypt unearthed an Achilles heel that couldn't be reconciled with the astronomical abrasion resistant claims made of early Spectra lines. I guess that if the non-fishing marketing people behind those brands figured that if the stuff could stop a bullet it must also be bullet proof in fishing situations. The assumption is both wrong and right. The issue lays in relativity. Were GsP lines the same diameter as the monofilaments they've replaced, abrasion resistance wouldn't be such an issue. But they're not; gel spuns are upwards of four times thinner

McBRAID

In an age when the majority of braids are badged by marketing companies following the out-sourced manufacture by a relative handful of makers, the McPherson family company stands as a lone exception. The world's longest established fishing lines manufacturer was established in 1898 when Scottish rope maker George Ross McPherson emigrated to Australia. For over a century, through times of cordage, catgut, nylons, dacrons, copolymers, and into the gel spuns era the Platypus Line Company has remained on the technology cutting edge. Dyneema and Spectra braids engineered and constructed at the Brisbane plant are amongst the longest established in today's market. There's no better place to develop and prove fishing lines than in a country surrounded by over 40,000 km of ocean. Australia also has some of the world's biggest and toughest freshwater fish.

Don McPherson was much liked and respected amongst the world lines community. He was that rare entity, a line maker able to cast alongside the best. An exceedingly generous person, the full extent of Don's giving may never be known. Professional affiliations were so often friendship based. He helped Jim Vincent create the Rio brand and bring it from boutique flylines to a major player that Sage ended up buying.

In a programme at his Brisbane works, Don set a goal of producing a better braid. The trial and error, tweaking and checks, involved technicians and credible anglers. An end result was that an eight carrier / eight pik construction that's proved every-which-way superior to lesser-count imports. The McPherson mix retains a round shape under pressure. The firmer cross section vastly improved handling, casting in the wind and long term spool life. A serendipitous consequence of the McBraid formula lay in the concertina effect of the weave, a welcome 8 per cent stretch.

for the same tensile strength. This raises a fishing fact of life in that the single most effective defence a fishing line can have against abrasive surfaces is diameter. It's a simple dynamic where the load is spread, thus dispersing the wear and tear, can rapidly develop under pressure into a fatal hot spot. Dyneema lines weren't—wisely—subject to extravagant claims and didn't stall in their marketplaces while public confidence was re-built.

Another revelation was that the throb of a working lure created enough rasp tension when riding over sunken rock for the contact to wear through a GsP line. Mind you, lures the size of toy submarines that went deep enough to get the bends, get a bit of a grip in the water.

Second Time Around

In the decade plus since Spiderwire first came to town, material advances include finer—and therefore more expensive—deniers of raw GsP yarn along with significant advances in the resins used in finishing compounds. Fisherfolk who've picked up their first rod in the meantime are somewhat spared those early days growing pains—but still need to work on line control. Time has eroded the myth and misinformation. Former critics are putting prejudice aside and giving gel spuns another chance.

The second generation gel spuns saw new names added to the lines lexicon. Spiderwire Mk II came out as Fusion, a coated variety. Around the same time Berkley launched Fireline—produced by a brilliantly simple and extremely cost effective process that became cocooned in a watertight patent.

As Fireline achieved a market dominance despite a springy texture and a faster wear rate than true braids, major players such as Stren stayed with monofilaments only to fall further behind. Some big re-shuffles of corporate deck chairs occurred specifically the Berkley acquisition of opposition trade names, and in turn, being

incorporated into a global tackle superpower called Pure Fishing. Rather than being single entities, the Spiderwire, Fusion and Fireline labels each has a stable of Pure Fishing brands.

States of Play

The inexorable spread of gel spuns through the known sportfishing world has seen an interesting trend emerge. Some reflection of a national character in what anglers want—and get—in gel spuns. As with monofilaments, no single type best handles all situations. Horses for courses. In America the message is delivered by quarter-horse. The bassman majority want instant, raw, 'sock it to 'em' power. Anglers into lunker largemouths cut their teeth on the heaviest reasonably castable monofilaments. Market trends suggest many are ready to give gel spuns another chance. An extra thou' or so in the diameter of their GsP line isn't a concern. Just so long as those hawgs can be bulldogged to the boat.

The Japanese have gone in the opposite direction. Homeland fixations with finesse presentations and bonsai'd fish result in the show ponies of the braids genre. Nippon Dyneema produces GsP in finer deniers that aren't on the export list. These are reflected in braids that set the bar when it comes to outright thinness.

The lines popular with the oz-fisho are the brumbies of the breed. Australia's wild horses are found from the alpine snowline to the edge of the Great Stony Desert. To go the distance despite the conditions is a quality not possessed by every GsP or gee-gee. A long spool life is a constant reassurance of money well spent.

The rest of the sportfishing world seems to follow American trends. The largemouth bass fisheries that have been established in Spain and South Africa drive those markets. Canada has vast cold water fisheries in river and lake. Some idea of the enormity of those trout, salmon, pike and smallmouth bass stocks can be gleaned from the amount of French on the packaging of American made product. In Canada, faites vous parlez le Français prevails over common sense. Consumer goods can't be sold without a bilingual presentation.

Brazil and Argentina have roughly similar land masses to the United States and Australia and are rich in rivers. Their sportfishing resources extend from the peacock bass, payara and dorado of the Amazon and Parana to the yard long sea run browns of windswept Patagonia. Portuguese and Spanish language fishing magazines are just as available as those in the English speaking world. In editorial content and advertising, gel spuns—mostly American made and comparatively expensive—are present. But the conversion rate amongst the millions fishing out of necessity will never be of religious dimensions.

The Pacu pulls like blazes. It's a South American river fish not all that dissimilar to permit.

Chapter FOUR

BETWEEN THE LINES

The first gel spun line had a showbiz debut. In a move part Star of Bethlehem and part Pied Piper, the Spiderwire people suspended a glittering black widow over their space at American boating and fishing shows. It had size and attitude to frighten the bejesus out of Indiana Jones but folks there forgot their arachnophobia to flock to its shadow.

Allied Signal had recently been licensed to produce gel spun polyethylene. They called it Spectra. To The Netherlands inventors and the rest of the world it is Dyneema. Same stuff. The new miracle fibre was being used extensively in body armour for police and the military. Allied Signal figured that if GsP could slow bullets it could stop any fish. So they dealt themselves a hand in the fishing line business.

Spiderwire targeted America's biggest line consumers—bass fishers. Their thing was hauling out them hawgs, eyed crossed and jaws dislocated. Be it gun, rod or car, the American way is predicated on overwhelming power. Hawg is American fisho lingo for largemouth bass, fish similar in size, habit and fight to the Australian yellowbelly.

The performance of Spiderwire Mark I didn't live up to the promise. Handling hassles were a major problem. The lack of body brought about by low carrier and pik counts gave users the willies. More strife, where there was any sort of wind, than Lady Godiva could have on a bad hair day.

Second generation gel spuns behaved better. However some processes went too far and the results were wiry.

The middle ground comes at a cost. All gel spuns aren't created equal. They are constructed through processes that vary in complexity, cost effectiveness and in the user friendliness and spool life of the finished line. Makers worldwide are outnumbered by brands. Just as many a Scotch whisky (of various vat and vintage) comes from the same distiller, there's nothing unusual about competing GsP lines being made at the same place and via the same process. The divergent paths along which marketing companies take their products begin there. In fishing for hearts, minds and your dollars, differences can be nothing more than a different colour and words on the packaging. There are single malts amongst gel spuns and there's moonshine.

Sometimes the only difference between braids is colour. Most brands are erected by marketing companies – far more numerous than actual makers.

TERMS

Carrier

An industry term that defines the number of strands of a specific denier that are used of in the construction of braided lines. The raw yarn is supplied in bulk spools that are mounted on braiding machines according to the specs of the line to be produced. The finer the denier the more it costs. Braiding machines can take up to 12 spools, however a 12 carrier braid becomes cost prohibitive while not delivering the same percentage quantum increase in performance and durability that an eight carrier braid delivers over three and five strand constructions.

Carrier counts are a major consideration for makers. The three carrier braids, comprising the bulk of what's available, are therefore less costly to produce. Under magnification they have a triangular cross section. Five carrier braids comprise a significant section of the market. They have pentagonal cross sections. Whilst those makers have little to gain by quoting low carrier count, there is commercial mileage in citing eight carrier lay-ups. Moreso as fisherfolk become better informed about lines composition. An eight carrier braid is superior every way. An octagonal cross section is as geometrically close as a braided line can be to perfectly round. It retains shape under pressure and has a considerably longer working life.

Pik

Another industry term used to define the tightness of the weave. When applied to braids, the pik count is based on the number of times per centimetre an individual strand meets an imaginary straight line along the outer surface of the line that's parallel to the core.

Again, eight is the magic number for GsP yarns, in that this provides an optimum 'concertina' buffer effect having in mind the basic brittle nature of the fibres. To reduce the pik content in a weave is to invite handling hassles. Conversely, raising pik levels to double figures and beyond lowers the impact threshold and reduces knot strengths. Very high pik lines are prone to fatigue problems due to the brittle nature of GsP fibres. An eight pik braid delivers the best of all worlds to anglers and has a serendipitous bonus in that it can deliver up to 8 per cent stretch.

Tom Evans on a black marlin - a #30 or #50 8 carrier/8 pik braid is backing of choice amongst big league flyrodders.

The various deniers used by fishing line makers should, but tend not to, reflect what fisherfolk pay. Anglers accustomed to the established monofilament market, where the manufacturing cost is mainly based on the quantities of raw material that go into the brew, express surprise on learning that less in a gel spun world can cost more.

Waxing Lyrical

Given their price structures, there'll always be a market for the bottom shelf gel spuns. This class of line is produced by twisting two or three strands of 'coarse' GsP yarn and applying a wax coating. They have a sticky feel that impedes casting. Backlashes become prevalent due to line stutter as it comes off a revolving spool. Those things become a worsening condition: so-so to so bad, so soon. The wax leeches from the fibres. With no bonding agent, the few loosely twisted strands comprising the line's foundation loses what little body it had. Telltale fluffing occurs as exposed fibres rupture. The line is doomed.

The false economy of these (generally) green coloured 'twist and wax' lines doesn't generate a lot of repeat business amongst thoughtful anglers.

Taking the Heat

Thermofused lines are cheaper and faster to produce than true braids. The manufacturing process sees gel spun fibres that have been arranged in parallel being drawn through a heating element. The fibres on the outside of the bundle melt, thus forming a coating. An accompanying degree of heat shrink makes thermo fused gel spuns the thinnest unknotted tensile strength to diameter ratio amongst the gel spuns. The thermofused genre has a wiry nature that becomes more pronounced as breaking strains increase, and a finish less durable than those of true braids.

Fused gel spuns are a very cost effective choice in single digit breaking strains. The type enjoys a major market share amongst fisherfolk swinging ultra light spin tackle. But as diameters increase a wiry texture becomes increasingly evident.

Coating the Pill

Coated gel spuns were an obvious next step when untreated first generation lines flopped. For the times they were a major improvement, inasmuch as they provided lines with much needed body. Coated gel spuns rely on the encapsulating effect of 'finish' compounds. To that end those chemical brews, which can be hot bath or cold dip, have an inter-strand connectivity that results in a stiffness that lies between that of thermofused and braided gel spuns. Another consequence is a degree of malleability in the finished line. This is due the number of strands comprising the line and the way they are arranged prior to the finish being applied. Under pressure on the reel, coated gel spuns exhibit a degree of flattening and take on a kinky nature. Some coatings have solid matte colours, others an opaque, mono like appearance. The type wears reasonably well though outlasted by true braids.

Braiders of the Lost Art

Some of today's finest gel spuns are produced on machines much older than the anglers using the lines they make. In order to be competitive, braiding companies operate around the clock. Braids produced through this slow, time worn technology still outlast and outperform any line we can get from modern science.

First generation braids were untreated and, having no body, were billowy in a breeze and generally behaved badly. It wasn't until carrier and pik counts were optimised, and finishing brews perfected, that braids solidified as the best all round choice for performance conscious anglers.

A second generation saw the emergence of higher carrier and pik counts. Though possessing fuller body, a characteristic that vastly improves handling and wear, their manufacture still proceeds at a snail pace on banks of machines that run twenty-four/seven. A handful of braiding companies manufacture the fishing world's many brands. The Japanese cottage commune system remains an exception.

Do more strands make a better braid? Absolutely! High carrier braids are superior in offering a more rounded cross section that retains shape under pressure and cope better with wear and tear. A reasonable analogy is to liken GsP lines to car tyres. From the moment they hit the road, tires—as our American mates spell the word—begin to wear. A multi-belt steel radial outlasts and generally outperforms those having a lesser reinforcement.

Low pik lines have a lace like texture and are contrary to handle. They flatter under pressure and dig into the spool. High pik braids have more body and offer better degrees of the user friendly. Eight is the magic number in that it creates a concertina effect that delivers cushion and stretch—priceless commodities in small measures. Ten piks are too many, overly compressing the weave and causing fatigue problems down the track.

Prior to spools of Spectra/Dyneema yarn being loaded onto the braiding machines, makers have to decide how many. This question may be determined more by profit considerations than a blueprint for the best possible line. The bottom line for braid is no different to any other manufacturing. Material costs are the first and major consideration. A four carrier braid can be produced faster and for less money than an eight carrier. The makers and marketers of eight carrier braids have realised the commercial advantage of citing body in product presentation. Four carrier braids have a square-ish format, five carriers have a hexagonal cross section. The octagonal shape of eight carrier braids is as near to round as technology can produce and is the secret of their superior handling and spool life.

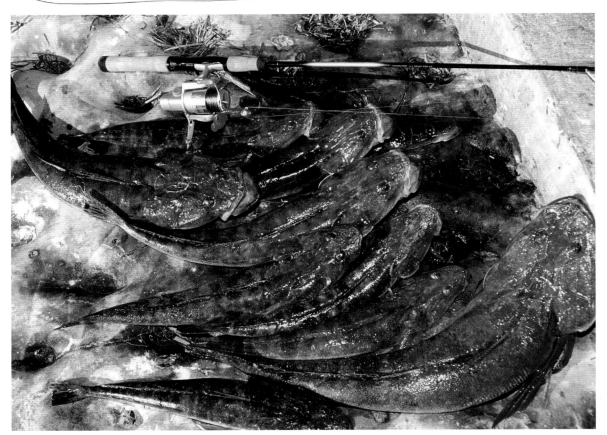

A fused gel spun is a cost effective choice for light spin work with lines under 10 pound stated breaking strain.

Carrier counts tend to be overlooked at a retail level but should be an issue for informed anglers.

A newer process produces what may be termed a radial braid. These are more time and cost effective to make than lines produced on traditional braiding machines. Their composition has a single strand that forms a central core, around which the other seven are woven. Though possessing the 'body' absent in loose weave braids, their longevity isn't equal to a high pik gel spun and is very much dependant on the bonding capacity of the finish brew—the mortar amongst the bricks.

Hybrids
Some braids have a mixed make up. Gel spun fibres are blended with polyester or braided around a monofilament core. Those makers see their product as a compromise that will appeal to anglers still suspicious or bedevilled by 100 per cent GsP make up. Hybrids offer both advantage and disadvantage in that diameter is thicker for a given strength.

Special Braids
The odd market niche has developed that calls for a special gel spun braid. A hollow variety marketed under the boutique Jerry Brown brand is in demand as a connecting component for 'wind-on' monofilament leaders, especially those used in heavy duty offshore jigging.

The Platypus Line Company won a major industry award for a sinking braid. This has found favour with anglers fishing with baits suspended under a float—the luderick community come to mind—and those lake situations where bubble floats offer a number of highly successful presentation methods for trout.

Skin Deep
The chemical treatments given lines after completion of the braiding process enhance handling and extend working lives. However the simple unadulterated truth remains that no treatment, pre or post braiding, potion or snake oil, makes either line or knots any stronger than the sum total of the fibres comprising the line.

These urethane based finish compounds contain Teflon and silicone additives along with the newer resins industry makes available. While permeating the innards of braided lines, those treatments still remain skin deep and do nothing to strengthen the line.

By the way, the compositions of those various brews are not national secrets. Rather, they are developed by a petrochemical industry that regularly keeps the braiding and textile people abreast of advances.

Colour

Colour has a number of functions. Some makers use colour, or lack thereof, as a camouflaging agent. Brown tinted lines are highly regarded by freshwater anglers fishing big rivers. Clear lines are the first choice of anglers stalking spooky fish in lakes. Some makers go the extra step and add a clouding agent that gives more of a matte, non-glint finish. Opaque and clear copolymers and fluorocarbons are in high demand for flyfishing leaders. As a companion product to some first generation braids, the same off-white as raw GsP yarn, brown and green 'camo' permanent markers were on the manifest at Bass Pro and Cabelas.

Optically enhanced lines are popular. Fluorescent pigments have a laser affect that aids situation awareness, especially in salt water. Hot pink provides the ideal each-way bet. In the breakdown of the light spectrum with depth, pinks become greys. There's also a body of scientific evidence to the effect that bright pink is beyond the vision register of many game fish.

Line makers use certain colours as a means of instantly identifying their product—and as a means of picking up de facto promotion. Those smart enough to be first with a distinctive colour that catches on, get a market jump before the copycats take heed. Magazine pictures of reels containing a recognisable brand are as good as paid advertising.

Multi-coloured braids are popular with deep-sea anglers. These are metered by different colours in the manner established by lead core trolling lines. An interesting variation on that has been adopted by deep-sea anglers using overhead reels not having a level wind mechanism and loaded with a single colour braid. When commencing a retrieve off the bottom, they build a little 'tell-tale' hump in the corner of their spool. This provides advance warning of the bottom proximity on their next drop.

Colouring agents are mixed in with finishing compounds and illustrate the fact that gel spun polyethylene fibres are impervious to chemical intrusion. At best, all treatments—whether pre or post braiding—are skin deep and will leech in time. Colour fade is the most tangible in the short to mid term. Colour loss has little impact in reducing tensile and knot strengths. Some braids still labouring away on my workhorse reels have reverted to the opaque white of the raw GsP fibres after a decade of use. The carrier count and pik rate of a braid can have more to do with colour loss and wear rates than chemical additives.

The colour coding used as a depth control for lead core trolling lines has been adopted by some braids.

For the Record

The International Game Fish Association has custody of angling records established via a line class system. The divisions extend from the 1 kg class—applicable to light spin tackle—through to the heavyweight 60 kg class employed in chair fishing for the biggest marlin roaming the world's oceans.

The monofilaments and dacrons used by anglers fishing to IGFA rules are rated by makers according to their class. Those designations are, in essence, a statement that the line will break within that division. Knots are called upon to hold at pressures as close as possible to cut off point into a higher division. The spirit of the endeavour is to spool up with a rated line that falls within the relevant line class division. And hope that a section used in the capture breaks within bounds when submitted along with the rest of the claim.

It was a matter of time before Spectra/Dyneema lines entered the IGFA arena. Risky business? Well, on the face of things, yes. As already stated, the knotting regime for monofilaments and dacrons gets close to 100 per cent of the unknotted strength of stated breaking strains. Anything better than 70 per cent in gel spuns is an excellent outcome.

One would think that percentage breaks of that order is giving too much away. But when test procedures for world record claims at IGFA's Fort Lauderdale headquarters are factored in, things fall into place—for makers and anglers, at least.

The time honoured procedure for line samples submitted for line class record claims is for verification on the most accurate line test equipment technology can provide. Prior to testing, the sample has to be anchored on the machine. But therein lies a problem for the pinch type arrangement that works so well with monofilaments—the pressure point thus created becomes the foundation for a rupture. State of the art digital equipment gets around the problem by using Nelson bollards, named after the British age of sail naval hero. A time and line consuming process—brought about by the multi wraps needed to eliminate creep, compression and the load on anchor points—provides outcomes on unknotted tensile strengths that are accurate within a decimal point.

The speed at which the load is applied has a major bearing. That set of physics invokes a Newton Law of Motion that is very relevant to knots and fishing lines. The IGFA calibration is for the load to be exerted at 400 mm per minute and applies to monofilaments that can have a 25+ per cent stretch. A variation that accommodates the comparative lack of stretch in gel spuns would need to be calculated from those tests.

At first the erratic and unpredictable knotting nature of gel spuns ruled them out for line class fishing, but other influences have been chipping away. Good knots or not, fisherfolk want that gel spun feel. Some also want their records.

Judy Gay and IGFA Hall of Famer Jack Erskine at the HIBT – an event from the golden era of gamefishing tournaments of the mono/ dacron age.

Chapter FIVE

REELY YOURS

While gel spuns are generally compatible with most reel types, the performance peaks that superlines deliver come at some additional cost. The pain before the gain hits the hip pocket nerve. Any old reel won't do, but that hasn't stopped folks spooling up relics from the shed, reels that are Chinese cheap or simply mechanically inadequate. When the line costs more than the reel, the marriage is in trouble right from the start. Irrespective of reels, fisherfolk have to work on line management; newlyweds moreso than the well adjusted. A bonus, though not one there to be abused, is the comparative absence of the line twist that long bedevilled mono filled spin reels. A purpose built reel is the key to a happy relationship.

Reel manufacturers have been making design concessions to accommodate gel spuns pretty much since day one. At the behest of American sporting goods wholesaler, JWA, French maker Mitchell came up with a rushed and radical criss-cross line laying concept for spin and baitcast reels intended as companion products for Spiderwire mark 1. They were as useful as an ashtray on a Harley Davidson.

The arrival of gel spuns has been a no-risk driver in a surge by major makers towards technical excellence. Much of the initial running was from Daiwa and Shimano, however other makers have caught on and closed the gap. Spinning reels had always been a middle of the road tool. Save for breakouts such as one led by Jack Erskine when he changed the face of light tackle billfishing with tuned Spinfishers, the mono age kept spin reels in their place. Not any more, micro

Lefty Kreh's globetrotting travels and extraordinary catch file is matched by his collection of fly, spin and casting reels.

A neat innovation that assists smooth casting is a chamfered spool lip.

REEL HISTORY

The 1960s were a significant epoch for reels. American sporting goods wholesaler Garcia acquired Pezon et Michel and anglicised the brand to Mitchell. The Mitchell 300 became a world best seller. The 410/411 was even better. When German tackle giant DAM came on the scene it was with spin reels possessing Panzer-like bullet proofing. A Garcia expansion saw the acquisition of distribution rights for the Swedish maker ABU. Founded in 1921 by Arne Borgstrom, Urfabriken (watchmaker) the company bearing those initials went on to make to produce the legendary Ambassadeur baitcasters. Those red warriors, the 5000 and larger 6000 dominated world sales. ABU also produced the credible Cardinal series of spin reels. These embodied the mechanical mistake of an internal drag system easily permeated by lubricants. Following a Mitchell/ABU/Garcia impasse the French maker went its own way.

In what was, in hindsight, a watershed event the emerging Daiwa Corporation purchased British reel maker Whyte-Hall during the mid 1960s. Along with brands like Intrepid and the J. W. Young Ambidex, Whyte-Hall enjoyed support in the UK and Australia, though never seriously challenging the European and Scandinavian brands. Amongst a variety of Australian made reels to have their hour in the Downunder sun, the Capstan Whirlaway was the Wirraway amongst the spin reel genre. Aviation buffs will recall the Wirraway

as the Australian made frontline fighter at the onset of World War II. It proved easy meat for the Japanese zero and cost good men before it could be replaced by the gutsier Kittyhawk. The gutsiest affordable spin reels are the American made Penn Spinfisher series. Though usable with gel spuns, there are limitations brought about by a narrow spool and the uneven line lay of reels straight from the box. It will be interesting to see where Penn goest now that corporate buy and sell sees the brand in the Pure Fishing conglomerate and manufacture in China.

Closed face spin cast reels are the least mechanically efficient fishing apparatus and are totally unsuited to gel spuns—and stresses beyond panfish. An enduring American popularity, especially through the southern states, is due to a one-step push button operation. A lake scene in Walk the Line with actors Reece Witherspoon and Joachim Phoenix—who sing better than they cast—underpins a simplicity of use.

Mitchell's biggest Australian sellers were the manual pick up #489/#499s that peaked during the boom days of kingfish jigging.

thin gel spuns take finesse presentations to new levels of finery. Whether a six inch Ayu, where the only sound is the gurgle of the stream, or a pitching deck and deep sea slugfest with a hundred pound amberjack that strains locomotive gears and a formula drag, spin reels are at the epicentre.

Irrespective of whether it's an over priced, jazzed up something from Japan, or an adequate reel made somewhere else, new degrees of tension—and. of

course, constant vigilance—predicate the loading and retrieval of gel spuns. It's a sliding scale—the tighter, the less trouble. A starting point involves significantly greater pressures that might have been acceptable with monofilaments. Few get it right first time.

Despite being super slippery, GsP has the innate capacity to snare itself. Monofilaments were never as wayward when left to their own devices. Spin reels are the more afflicted and therefore a precise line

Reels with an uneven line winding mechanism are best left for monofilaments.

laying mechanism is mandatory One that feeds even, concentric layers across the entire spool. Reel makers not attending to that fine tuning do so at their peril.

Angler oversight and error shares responsibility for those frustrating snarls. At cast velocities, shock waves form as the line comes off the spool. A bottleneck effect at the stripping guide, and sometimes a subsequent runner, results in the second or third of those catchy undulations overtaking the one ahead. A simple loop forms…then locks back on itself. The rest falls into place like an end to end freeway pile up. Over-filled spools, loosely retrieved line and jerky rod loading are contributing factors as is bad rod design and bulky bridged guides. Single foot types offer the most trouble free line passage. It's significant that the Fuji K guide has been specifically developed for braids. Another remedy lies with full bodied high carrier braids that are less inclined to waft around. The impetus of a cast with spin gear can drag those snarls beyond the rod tip. With baitcasters they occur at spool zero. Castus interruptus is a double whammy that eats up valuable fishing time and costly line.

The Fuji K-guide has been designed to eliminate the snarls that happen with spin reels spooled with braids.

The incidence of slack line can be reduced if spin reels are cued so the bail arm rotor engages on the down stroke. Reels last longer when bail arms are engaged manually.

Fixed or Revolving Spool?

There was a time when spin and baitcast reels each had their place. Not any more. For a couple of generations—reels, not ours—spin has been chipping away at what many have considered the turf of the overhead. The uptake of gel spuns has spurred reel makers towards excellence in engineering and ergonomics just as an Englishman at a late 19th century Manchester textile mill took inspiration from bobbins for a concept for a fishing reel.

Questions between the two—as to which is best—tend to be clouded by perceptions and ideology.

The issue of accuracy lies at the forefront. For yonks, bass fishers and the ilk have held the conviction spin reels can't match baitcasters for pinpoint presentations. Not so! A good spin man can match casts with the best—but needs better reflexes than the average baitcast user. Because of start-up inertia and the revolving spool having to get up to speed, lures launched from spin gear have a higher initial velocity and therefore require more control at distances inside those of which the tackle is capable.

Reels with revolving spools have always had the edge when it comes to winching power. The gap widens as reels get bigger. Imagine the dimensions of crown wheel and pinion gearing needed were spin reels ever to be successful on thousand pound marlin. Two hundred pounders are a different matter though. Innovative engineering, gutsier gearing and drag pressures once the

province of lever drag game fish reels have widened the scope of big, purpose-built spin reels to include oceanic middleweights.

The lightweight end of the tackle spectrum has always been where the overall versatility of spin reels comes to the fore. As lure weights get below $1/4$oz (7 gram) baitcast reels become impracticable. Neither do they deliver the distance of spin, but the backlash bogey is well and truly out of the bottle. A crochet needle is a handy tool for such contingencies.

Under slung is under sung. A very pertinent point that gets overlooked in spin verses plug discussions is the lessened physical effort required for a reel that hangs under the rod, pendulum like, compared with one above that needs a support grip to maintain comfort and balance. Necessity being the mother of invention, low profile baitcasters had a genesis there. In the eyes of most dual users, the comparative physical effort with bass calibre casting tackle has an infinitesimal difference, however, spin offers a no-risk ease of use advantage when the rod is used to work jigs and jink minnows. A big day at sea is another matter. Working a one pound (500 gram) knife jig in a hundred fathoms sees the blokes who've saddled themselves with overheads taking longer breaks.

There's absolutely no doubt that at the end of a big day's casting, anglers saddled with spin can cover more water while using less muscles than their baitcaster brethren.

It's very much an open question whether braids will see the sun set on monofilaments and dacrons for big game reels.

SPIN Vs BAITCAST

Was a time it was fashionable to look down upon anyone using a spin reel. Not anymore. Developments in spin reels and skill levels of users have reached a point where differences are too close to call.

	Spin	Baitcast
Cost	★★★★★	★★★★☆
Innovation	★★★★★	★★★☆☆
Cosmetics	★★★★☆	★★★★★
Ease of operation	★★★★★	★★★☆☆
Line Capacity	★★★★☆	★★★★☆
Mechanical efficiency	★★★★☆	★★★★★
Drags	★★★☆☆	★★★★★
Retrieve speeds	★★★★★	★★★★☆
Casting distance		
(light weights)	★★★★★	★★★☆☆
(med/heavy weights)	★★★★☆	★★★★★
Casting accuracy	★★★★☆	★★★★★
Range of line sizes	★★★★★	★★★★☆

Relative tooling costs and production time sees a blowout on the side of spin. Some spin mills go for a grand. That's too much money when one considers that four reels each costing a quarter as much can, collectively, last longer. In the charter school of hard knocks, at least.

Spin reels are the main beneficiaries of the design and material updates needed to accommodate gel spuns. But baitcasters take the cake for cosmetics. Apart from low profile designs that better fit the palm, the newer packages haven't a lot that's not whistles and bells. Spin reels involve more movements to cue and cast. Baitcasters, by and large, are fitted with a thumb bar spool release, a one touch cue. An educated thumb can take some teaching, so too, the finesse forefinger needed to get the best from spin.

Low profile baitcasters can be a bit shy on line capacity, the same goes for shallow spool spin reels, both products of a Japanese bonsai mentality. Major makers hedge the bet, thankfully, with realistic capacities. The mechanical efficiency of the fixed spool concept has almost caught up with that of revolving spool reels. Almost. Ditto drags.

As for outright speed, the spool diameter and speedier gearing makes spin packages the winner. When it comes to casting lure weights of under 5/16ths oz (10 grams), spin is the only real choice but as weights increase things even out. For heavyweight casting, say weights of 2 oz (55grams) and over, an overhead reel can cast further.

In the right hands, a spin reel can be just as accurate as a baitcaster. However, because the lure initially travels faster when the cast is released the anglers using spin need good control to compete. Spin reels have an ascendancy when it comes to handling fine gauge gel spuns but as diameters increase, the revolving spool reels come more into their own.

A Spin Short List

These features in a spin reel enhance compatibility with gel spuns.

Wide and Skirted Spools

The so-called long cast spools are an innovation that has been widely adapted by industry. Being wider, the retrieved line is spread more evenly across the spool and casting distance is thus increased through a reduction in friction as the lure is in flight. However the technology has taken a further step, wringing a bit more distance from the concept by tweaking the rotor and bail arm oscillation to provide a subtle taper to the line plug. A design innovation that dates back to the late 1960s, skirted spools eliminate that line twist around the base of the rotor that's caught a lot of us at some time or other. Another spin development is a spools lip chamfer.

Being Shafted

Where possible purchase reels that have a handle that screws into the central crank shaft. This setup amounts to better engineering and is generally a feature of top of the range models. The alternative arrangement, where the crank shaft is attached to the handle assembly and things are secured on the opposite side by a threaded screw, is satisfactory for a time. Prolonged use results in a degree of slack movement, a worsening condition, developing in the lynchpin region.

Bail Arm Blues

Spin ergonomics have moved towards a contoured 'line trap' bail arm that locates and maintains the line under pressure. Line rollers have been upsized in the facelift given the spin format. Large line rollers offer more bearing surface and are needed to compensate for the slippery nature of gel spuns.

A crisp bail arm recovery is a good indication of a robust reel. When using spin reels, get in the habit of closing the bait arm manually. The working life of the reel will be extended by saving stress to the trip mechanism and the hinge connecting handle and crank shaft.

Quite apart from mechanical considerations, there are a couple of bonuses to be had by manually engaging the bail while the lures in is the late stages of flight.

The straightening line tends to remove those annoying and potentially disastrous loops that sometimes become trapped on the spool as the retrieve gets underway.

Thinking anglers with the reflexes position themselves for a reaction strike by initiating a skittering or fleeing motion immediately the lure splashes down. Fish aren't that keen on lures that fall from the sky on a piece of string, sink a bit and then waddle off. Time enough to cool a blood rush.

Bite detection becomes much more acute with modern reels and braids.

American maker, Quantum—these days thinking beyond bass—has developed thinner titanium bail arms along with an engage/disengage system that is magnetic rather than mechanical.

In Drag

A spool mounted drag is an imperative. Avoid reels having an internal drag system. Squeezed in amongst other innards, internal breaking systems aren't to be taken seriously. Besides mechanical inefficiency, the mechanism is far too susceptible to the intrusion of lubricants. Contrary to some popular belief, oil and grease seriously erode drag smoothness and capability.

Getting a Grip

Wherever possible, settle for reels with handles that screw into the horizontal drive shaft. Many designs incorporate the drive shaft into the handle assembly by way of a lynchpin hinge. Collapsible handles aren't for our convenience. The fold down concept is all about packaging and freight…more boxes in a carton, more cartons in a shipping container.

Daiwa and Shimano have brought out some new handle designs for their saltwater heavyweights. Some are golf ball shaped and nearly as big, others are a T-bar similar to a car gear shift lever. Their purpose is to provide more purchase for anglers who might need a bit more cranking grunt. The trend is taking hold in middleweight reels where it is an intrusive and unnecessary overkill.

Bearings and Bushes

The quality, or otherwise, of a spin reel can be gauged by the number of (ball) bearings it contains. Some top shelf models have upwards of a dozen. The higher the count the more the reel costs, the smoother it runs and the longer it lasts. Bearings are mounted at strategic load bearing locations, critically on the crank shaft. A cheaper alternative for manufacturers is to use brass or nylon bushes. These wear rapidly and represent false economy.

The Need for Speed

A long existing trade-off with spin reels deals with speed and stress. The faster the gear ratio the more strain on gears and bearings. Those limitations imposed an upper retrieve ratio of 6:1. Depending on the spool diameter, a six to one reel brings in as much as five feet of line per turn of the handle. High retrieve speed reels are in demand by anglers casting to breaking fish. Schools of oceanic nomads like tuna have a competitive streak that's triggered by a hot retrieve, but in hard fished waters they can be boat shy. Gel spuns add yards to casts. Smart anglers capitalise on the extra distance by keeping the boat away where it less likely to spook the school.

Anglers in that swim may not have unlimited opportunities to cast at breaking fish and need a rapid recycle rate to get as many casts in as possible. Fast reels are handy for burning lures back through unproductive stretches. Those zones exist in both horizontal and vertical places. It's a long way to the top for a slow coach

A world record 10-1 Yellowfin Tuna taken by Gregory Clarke during a golden age for lever action reels and IGFA rated monofilaments.

reel when fish are glued to a reef 200 metres down. Gel spuns make jig fishing such depths a reality on a calm day.

Speed Also Kills

Amongst reasons why anglers aren't hooking more inshore and freshwater fish like bass, bream, barramundi, snook and sea trout is that they are cranking too fast. It's a habit that requires conscious effort to break and vigilance to thereafter maintain. Out of sight can be out of mind for fish that aren't on the prod, a condition that occupies a fair slice of their day. Reels with a mid-range retrieve ratio (4.2:1 to 5.2:1) are a better choice for anglers not having the discipline to slow a speed machine down to a dawdle, and the heavy-handed who grind away without using the rod.

If anything, I'd err on the side of speed and learn to slow down when the situation demands. There are cheap brands out there with stamped gears that churn at a 3.7:1 rate. Don't even go there.

Trigger Fingers and Educated Thumbs

Left hand or right? That's a question that fisherfolk inclined towards spinning reels have been asking for over half a century and will continue to do so. There's no single monosyllable answer.

The notion that if you cast right handed you should wind the reel with your left hand evolved from flyfishing for trout. The idea is that you don't have to switch hands, your strongest hand stays on the rod. It's not an unreasonable argument. If you're not after strong fish that run long distances and slug it out for extended periods, it doesn't make much difference with which hand a young man reels. They become adept at using either for other high-priority functions.

However, if you hook fish that are going to tear off a lot of line and argue with you for some time, there's a powerful case for reeling with your dominant hand.

To extrapolate that definition, this is what a fishing neurosurgeon told me. We really do our watch repairs and delicate tinkering with a specific hand. And wield the blacksmith hammer in the other. Translated into spin-speak, the index finger of the 'tinkerer' is best employed controlling the line while the rest of the hand does the rod. The hammer hand is—and can be—best trained to do the cranking.

Many who advocate not using the dominant hand claim they can use a spinning reel with the non-dominant hand and have no problem—and they won't, for two reasons. A single turn on the handle on a spinning results in the bail arm travelling at least four revolutions, more with the fast movers. However, the main reason you can efficiently wind spinning reels with the non-dominant hand is that the turning arc of the handle is huge when compared to a baitcaster or fly reel. Think about it—how many right handed fishermen wind plug casting reels with the non-dominant hand? Almost none.

Much is made that the dominant hand 'is more co-ordinated' when winding a reel in tight turns. It's also true that winding with the dominant hand on strong, long running fish provides the angler with more endurance.

A true test is to do a timed recovery of 50 metres of line using either hand. You'll never do as well with the non-dominant hand. Endurance and the kind of fishing you do are reasons enough to keep winding with your dominant hand. Spin reels make it easy on anglers by offering an easy conversion.

If things were that simple there'd be more left handed baitcasters around. Unlike left handed rifles and golf clubs, which still share some common componentry with those for the rest of the world, keeping the Molly-Dookers happy involves a complete reverse tooling. Respected makers like ABU have responded to demands and produced some left handed models, but it's hard not to conclude that the industry keeps hoping that the problem will either fix itself or go away.

Jack Erskine demonstrates perfect form with a heavy duty baitcaster.

The baitcaster was once the hallmark of experienced bassmen. But not anymore.

A plug for baitcasters

Baitcast reels have gone down the same track as cars. The old ABU red warriors that I first learned to drive were sparse between handle and spool. Quick to pull down and easy to fix, not that they often needed fixing. Points and carburettor stuff, kinda. But take a look under the bonnet now…so many bits crammed between key and tyre, handle and spool. You'd better know what you're doing before taking to any of it with a spanner.

It goes without saying that the same even and tight line spread across the entire spool width is a critical prerequisite for prolonged, trouble free casts. Though speed humps rather than hills, the undulations forming in gel spuns at cast velocities are still prone to locking back on themselves. Educated thumbs and reels calibrated commensurate with skill levels generally keep things under control. But there's always the unforeseen. Bulky braid to mono leader knots are the root cause of a baitcaster bugaboo for which there's no known cure. As the connection travels through the rod guides, it may judder its way rather than fly smoothly. Though nanosecond contacts, those little stutters are the seeds of a backlash.

From little things, big things grow. How true the homily. Leader lengths have a lot to do with the frequency of the problem. Shorter leaders and low profile connections with a smooth outer surface are amongst the solutions.

Good as they were, and some undoubtedly still are, older generation baitcast reels do not contain the engineering that will produce a perfectly level line distribution and thus dramatically reduce gel spun backlashes. The newer generations alleviate the problem with vee shaped spools and/or tapered spool shoulders. These encourage the retrieved line to lay against the spool flange rather than forming the edge gaps familiar to baitcast lifers.

Unless I'm missing something, innards that have gone from mechanical to magnetic to computer chips seem over-engineered. Change for the sake of change, something new to release at next year's tackle show. One example of implications for gel spuns lies with level wind mechanisms that disengage as the spool unloads during a cast or under drag. The non-fishing design bureau people may feel inclined to pat themselves on the back for yet another technical advance. The fact of the matter is that while this may add a couple of yards to the cast—may—it upsets the index between level wind and spool. The resulting acute angles at the level wind gate are a source of wear, especially for thermofused gel spuns.

Conversely, the old style level wind mechanisms that continue to traverse as line comes off the reel are an insignificant penalty when it comes to casting distance.

Ergonomics have changed with innards. The old round shapes are in the background these days as newer low profile models take over the spotlight. They sit lower on the rod and can be more comfortably accommodated in the palm.

How much line?

Anglers filling reels for the first time are well advised to dwell on that question. Given the cost of gel spuns and the fact that there's usually left over yardage from store bought spools, the urge is to cram on as much as possible. That's a mistake! Bear in mind that the reel is already packing twice that quoted in mono based specs. A swag of line management problems that'll otherwise occur are eliminated when casting reels are underfilled by a couple of millimetres. Modern reels have a 'high tide' mark circumscribed on their spools.

Gel spun top shots are a popular and cost effective option that the market accommodates with 125/150 yard spools. Where line capacity isn't an issue, reel cores can be filled with mono as a permanent fixture. Apart from making a good bed, light monofilaments stretch while being loaded and cling to the spool edges thus filling those annoying gaps that develop in reels not in synch.

Beginners over-filling their baitcaster spools invite backlash.

Technology seems to be going too far with baitcasters. An implication for gel spuns lies with level wind mechanisms that disengage as the spool unloads during a cast or under drag. The non-fishing design people may feel inclined to pat themselves on the back for yet another technical advance. The fact of the matter is that while this might add a metre or so to the cast it alters the index between level wind gate and spool. The acute angles that result are a source of wear, especially for thermofused gel spuns. Conversely, the old style level wind mechanisms that continue to traverse as line comes off the reel are an insignificant penalty when it comes to casting distance.

When spooling reels equipped with level wind mechanisms, side pressure from one's fingers can assist the line to pack into the spool flanges. Ditto fly reels, where as extra precaution against gel spuns digging under pressure can be undertaken by making regular cross hatches. Those braids with the round cross-section that comes from an eight carrier construction are the only types worth considering as fly reel backing.

This conversion rate may help in calculating the amount of backing needed for fly reels being upgraded from Dacron to gel spuns.

#30 and #50 gel spuns are popular choices

#30 gel spuns are the equivalent of 2.4 times that of 20 pound Dacron.

#50 gel spuns are between 1.8 times and 2.0 times that of 30 pound Dacron.

This seems a good time to dynamite the myth associated with springy lines, misleading advice that is being peddled in support of thermofused gel spuns. Their alleged tendency to jump off the spools of spinning reels is cited as increasing casting distance. Not true! The extra friction created by line slap against runners and blank, costs rather than provides, additional yards. Smooth rod loading, spool design and rod runner type and placement are the things that really count.

Despite engineering advances, an educated thumb remains the most efficient anti-backlash control.
It works best when applied to lower spool edge rather than across the whole.

FOUNDATIONS

Some smart retailers realise the implications of sloppy spool up jobs and offer a service with braid sales.

The DIY approach takes time and effort and can be a time bomb if not done properly. The next fish of a lifetime lost through 'line dig' won't be the first.

Step one is to securely anchor the line. Otherwise slippage occurs and the entire line plug will rotate on the spool arbor like a car tyre on a loose fitting rim. Some modern baitcast reels have drilled spool arbours but their sharp edges suggest the holes are a weight saving measure rather than being there for angler convenience—those on my Daiwa CVZ 203 and 253 Millionaires too easily sever gel spuns to be used.

Amongst sound suggestions is to make several wraps around the arbor, cinch down with a six or seven turn uni-knot and apply a drop of super glue. Though forming a surface bond, there's enough surface area in the contact to provide sufficient shear strength to hold in light spin situations. For heavier duty applications, a couple of wraps of duct tape around the arbour will ensure the gel spun beds down into a solid foundation.

Building on a good start, it becomes an ongoing imperative to load gel spuns evenly and under higher tension. This can be a laborious task better suited to plumbers than pastry cooks, but absolutely necessary. A simple method that works with all reel types is to mount the reel on a rod and the dispensing spool on a screwdriver and apply pressure through a damp dishcloth as it rotates. It doesn't hurt to run the line through the stripping guide, but otherwise have both spools in a straight line. You'll find that a teenager can apply the brakes better than a grown man can crank.

My preference is first fully fill reels with finger pressure then (on a day when the traffic is light, grin) trail it all behind the boat and crank on some revs. Under an even 'guitar string' tension braids pack down to a more functional and less troublesome working level.

A quick Google search found all sorts of devices for spooling line, like this handy little jigger that's also easy on the budget.

Chapter SIX

NOT NOT KNOT RESPONSIBLE

el spuns have resulted in the biggest shake up in knotology since Noah anchored the Ark. A lot of it ado about the perception rather than the reality. No one's saying so, especially the marketers behind today's many brands, but the intent in overstated breaking strains is to factor in knots. You see, the best efforts by knotologists have around a 70 per cent consistency while 50 per cent might be all to expect from folk challenged by shoelaces and ties. With compelling logic, makers therefore cover that contingency by overstating unknotted breaking strains by 50 per cent and

sometimes more. Worse case scenario is users still have what it says on the box.

There are more knots out there than what might be untangled from a Roman orgy. Knots remain fishing's most subjective topic. Compounding the confusion is the fact that unlike situations with monofilaments, where a bad knot stands out like a set of Rotto nuts on a Chihuahua, with braids you'd never know. It's not widely realised, let alone accepted, that variations upwards of 30 per cent exist with any specific knot, depending on how it is tied, and by whom.

HOW AND WHY KNOTS FAIL

Gel spun fibres are subject to compression and creep. Those conditions are locked into the DNA of the material. Gel spun fibres are self-lubricating with the coefficient of friction of Teflon. Compression and elongation occurs at the pressure points knots create. Movement within knots tied in monofilament can be arrested by good formation and sound tightening. Not so with gel spun lines.

In a fatal boa-like cycle, creep follows compression as loads increase. Events reach a critical mass as crush pressures within knots continue to reduce the cross section of the core strands thereby encouraging further slippage.

Monofilaments have stretch factors ranging from 10 per cent to 30 per cent. Elongation occurs—in varying degrees—along the entire the entire molecular chain of the stressed section. On the other hand—and notwithstanding the 3.5 per cent stretch of raw gel spun fibres—elongation occurs at the immediate site of a pressure point, and to a negligible degree beyond, thus putting in motion a fatal train of events.

When re-constructing the breakdown of knots, the speed at which the load is applied is a vital yet overlooked factor. The everyday angler is more familiar with Murphy's Law than those of Sir Isaac Newton. Hasty conclusions blame the line rather than objectively assessing all the forces involved. These can be hazy enough with monofilaments let alone a far more complex material like GsP—but do not alter the fact that anglers break more lines than do fish.

Although not altering outcomes, the makers of top shelf braids are able to build some stress absorbing cushion into their products. One process is to pre-resin fibres prior to braiding. This prioritises the mortar and not the bricks. The other relies on the concertina effect of an 8 carrier / 8 pik construction.

Whatever the process, neither chemicals nor construction increase tensile strengths beyond the sum total of fibres comprising the line. Nor do they raise knot thresholds.

Other sections of the angler community, comfortable with mono and hand-me-down knots from grandpa's day, regard rigmaroles touted for gel spuns with the same suspicion directed at motorised buggies when they began replacing the horse. Aren't those cowboy movie bits great when everyone ducks whenever there's a backfire? Those folks came around though, and soon became accustomed to the foibles of the internal combustion engine.

Gel spuns bring some core issues into focus. Foremost is the fact that 100 per cent knots achievable in monofilaments are no longer possible. For reasons already, and to be, discussed outcomes over 70 per cent are an excellent outcome.

Then there's the matter of what knot(s) are best for a specific task. The swag of contenders on the roster can be culled to a handy half-dozen. Once learned, and users adjust to different handing qualities, gel spuns grow into one's hands like power steering.

Them's the Breaks

When it comes to testing tensile strengths, knots and line samples submitted for records, gel spuns involve physics that are somewhat different to those governing monofilaments. Results are difficult, if not impossible, to precisely quantify with current equipment and test regimes. Test apparatus ranges from backyard scales, to digital line test machines costing thousands—which haven't any opinions.

Whether crude or sophisticated, current equipment is wanting. Major problems arise at anchor points, either in the fallibility of whatever knot is used to secure the gel spun to the test equipment or arresting the indefinite slippage that occurs as the load increases. The usual set up with line test machines is pinch arrangements that secure both ends of the test sample. These are operated by a threaded screw, but due to the super slippery nature of gel spuns the creep alluded to elsewhere will develop into hotspots at pressure points. To get a 100 per cent accurate reading on gel spuns, tests need to be conducted without pressure points deteriorating into weak spots as loads increase. Mission impossible?

The closest technology gets is to fit oversize bollards to state of the art line test equipment around which multi-wraps are made prior to the load going on. Even then, the procedure only partially arrests the slippage and the development of fatal hot spots at pressure and anchor points.

To Be or Knot to Be

The secret in knotting gel spuns is to compensate for slippage and dissipate stress before it compounds in an area to form a hot spot.

There are a number of steps that will help towards delivering maximum strength:

• Wherever possible tie knots with the line doubled. In general terms, increasing the bearing surface spreads the load and trebles the wear, but for gel spuns a doubled line provides a lessening effect on the deformation of key strands in the core of the knot as compression and creep occur. Knots are stronger whenever the diameter of their helical coil can be increased.

• With knots that are formed by wrapping the tag end around the mainline, use at least twice the number of wraps that would be used to tie that knot in monofilament,

• Use the knots where the crossover made by the tag end is located at the rear rather than the front of the knot.

Handy Hints

Some enviable people have the talent to look at a line drawing and tie the knot right first time. Most of us do better after being shown by someone already accomplished. Thereafter, diagrams and photos become easier to interpret. As tying procedures take root, the structure of knots and the rationale of doing things that way will make better sense.

Don't scrimp on knots. Allow a sufficiently long tag end for proper formation of knots and, most importantly, to permit an effective grip in the tightening process. Gel spuns under load are capable of cutting careless fingers.

As a matter of course, fisherfolk are better served by being modest rather than miserly about line usage when rigging. Knots in gel spuns require more tension to tighten than anglers are accustomed to with monofilaments. Plumbers make better knot tighteners than pastry cooks but still require a sufficient tag end to get a proper grip. To harp on the point, wrapping gel spuns around fingers is risky business. I use a small screwdriver that's a fixture amongst my tools. A dozen wraps—yes you need that many to avoid slippage—eats up a few inches. An untold benefit of line usage at the business end, where the wear is greatest, is that line is being replaced before it becomes a liability.

Many anglers acquire the sort of dexterity that would allow them to tie a repertoire of knots while wearing boxing gloves. Others have trouble imprinting the muscle memory. The best possible foundation for a knot comes maintaining tension on the main line. One way is to place the rod in a holder and tighten the drag so the reel will not surrender line.

Fishing knots require that the line be bent, wrapped or looped and that at some stage the tag end line will cross over the main line in one or more places. A desired result is that once tightened by the angler, no further slippage occurs under fishing pressures.

A good way to approach knots in gel spun lines is to think in terms of traffic roundabouts rather than straight through intersections. By doubling the number of wraps and positioning crossovers to the rear, anglers are building a capacity within the knot to absorb and negate stresses that'd otherwise compound at key pressure points.

Words of Caution

Anglers yet to familiarise with lines so thin, yet strong, sometimes learn the hard way. Mostly it is a cut finger while tightening a knot or pulling a lure free from a snag. But sometimes it's a broken rod. To avoid those accidents, never try to budge a hung up lure by bending the rod. Rather, point the rod directly and the source and maintain a straight pull. If that doesn't work, use a hand towel for protection and make several wraps before trying again. Stubborn lures are more apt to come free when pressure is applied from the opposite direction, the longer the slant range, the better.

Tasks and Suggestions

In a mono world there are many knots that'll do the same job. Properly tied and tightened in the same material, they'll cope with pressures that are much of a muchness. While this substantially remains the case with gel spuns, there are factors both internal and external that advantage a certain knot or rig for a specific situation.

Knot to be outdone

Once anglers learn to tie knots while wearing gloves and (grin) having a hip flask handy for those cold, dark nights, questions remain. What knots serve best with braids? For this rig or that job? An oldie but a goodie or something new? The tangled rosters in the knot books—however exquisitely presented—can leave one none the wiser. No fault of the authors, just an understandable carryover from mono days. In a braids world, where knot thresholds are lowered to a common denominator, new criteria enter the equation. Whether fresh water or salt, bream or billfish, the knots regime can be distilled to a handful offering superior simplicity, security and, above all, functionality. There specific tasks and suggested shortlist are representative.

Task

To make a loop to facilitate attaching leaders

Knots and ratings

☆☆☆	Bimini Twist
☆☆☆☆	Australian Plait
☆☆☆	Quickie Double

Comments

Doubles are a hand me down from mono days when they could ensure a 100 per cent strength. The best bimini might deliver 70 per cent. Might. A greater certainly is that the knot creates the weakest link in the chain—right there—for no gain.

The Australian plait is marginally stronger but a lot more time consuming to tie. It is popular amongst the bream boys and for other ultra light spin situations.

The quickie double is a multi turn (four to six turns) overhand knot that's fast, safe and considering the reserve powers of gel spuns, just as strong.

HARRO'S QUICKIE DOUBLE

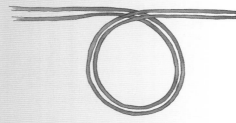

Double the length of gelspun line so that the doubled section is about 10cm longer than the required loop size.

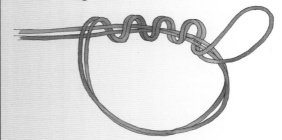

Form a loop with the doubled line to just above the tag end.

Make a four turn overhand knot and pull tight smoothly.

Task

Connecting single strand leaders

Knots and ratings

☆☆☆☆	Back to back Uni Knots ultra light tackle
☆☆☆	Back to back Uni Knots medium tackle
☆	Back to back Uni Knots heavy tackle
☆☆	Albright Knot
☆☆☆	Decky Knot
☆☆☆	Slim Beauty
☆☆☆	Fingertrap Knot
☆☆☆☆	Harro Knot

Comments

The efficiency of back to back uni-knots is excellent for connecting light mono leaders but its efficiency declines as diameters become disproportionate. A strength maximum happens when tied with the braid doubled and at least five turns are employed. The turns ratio of the mono can be reduced from four to three with heavier leaders.

The Albright is actually an extended version of the Sheet Bend of nautical use. Unmodified versions are subject to slippage and unravelling

The Fingertrap Knot came to life amongst Japanese anglers hucking coke can sized chuggers at giant trevally. It came from the need to form a connection that wouldn't derail during the explosive energy generated as a full blooded cast is unleashed. It is the slimmest of all connections and will not fail if properly tied.

Those steps require some dexterity and faith in ones knotology.

The slim beauty began life as a saltwater flyfishing connection in the Florida Keys spiritual home. It was introduced to the South Seas by Australia's saltwater fly supremo Dean Butler where it spread to lure fishers. While providing doubtless holding, a downside that shows itself now and again is the judder passage of the two exposed spirals of heavier leader material.

THE HARRO KNOT

Step 1: Fold the gel spun in half and wrap the loop three times around the leader material.

Step 2: Fold the leader material over and continue (in the same direction) with a further four wraps with the gel spun loop over BOTH strands of the leader material.

Step 3: Reverse the direction of the wraps and, commencing between the first and second set of wraps and working in the same direction, make a further four wraps. Then insert the gel spun loop under and between the first and second of the original wraps, making sure the gel spun loop exits between the folded leader material.

Step 4: Begin tightening by firstly pulling on the standing end of the leader. Then utilising the gel spun loop and positioning it at right angles to the knot, use finger pressure or a smooth implement like a screw driver shaft to further tighten the knot. Finally, use thumb and forefinger pressure to snig the knot tightly into the apex of the fold in the leader material.

Step 5: Bend the standing end of the leader material to facilitate the removal of the mono tag flush with the end of the gel spun wraps. Leave tag ends of a couple of millimetres in the gel spun. This is insurance against unravelling. Gel spuns do not always seat with the certainty and permanence of monofilaments.

Every which way, this is the superior gel spun/heavy mono leader connection.

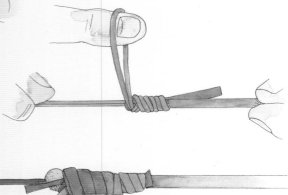

Task

Attaching pre-made looped leaders

Knots and ratings

☆☆☆☆ Loop 2 Loop Knot

☆☆☆ Harro Knot

Comments

The Loop 2 Loop connection ensures a 'square' knot whereas a single interlock can see the gel spun slip and morph into a girth hitch that will cut under pressure. The connection firstly requires a double in the braid. Irrespective of whether this is formed with a bimini twist or the simpler and just as strong six turn overhand knot, the inescapable fact remains that the weakest link in the system will be at the site of the knot.

LOOP 2 LOOP KNOT

The Loop2Loop knot adds a measure of security to braid to braid and braid to mono connections that employ end loops. The standard (once through) way of doing things —long entrenched in flyfishing circles—is risky as the gel spun can slide to form a girth hitch which will cut. The additional interlock supplied by the Loop2Loop connection eliminates this failing. It can be a bit picky to undo, but the peace of mind it otherwise provides is worth the trouble.

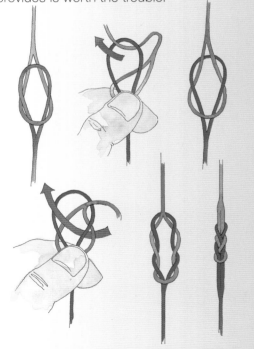

Task

Attaching single strand leader material to hardbody lures with fixed tow points, jigheads and flies. The freedom of movement afforded by a non-slip loop dramatically improves swimming actions.

Knots and ratings

☆☆ Perfection Loop

☆☆☆☆ Lefty's Loop

☆☆☆☆ Harro's Loop Knot

Comments

Shown to me by Dan Byford, this variation of Lefty's Loop has become (with no input from me!) known in Australia as Harro's Loop. Once formed, it morphs into a tidier loop by simply tightening the leader mainline. Loop knots need to be kept to a minimum hoop size. Dangers otherwise afoot might include the leading treble fouling in the loop or a stray twig. Loop knots are, but should not be, used on the split rings fitted to the two link of some lures. A jam knot is a better safeguard against the leader working its way inside split rings.

HARRO'S LOOP KNOT

This variation of a non-slip loop knot rates at over 90% and forms a superior knot that tightens easier. Ideal for attaching your leader to a lure or fly.

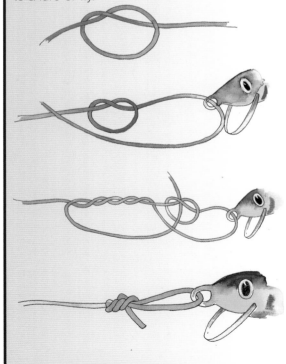

Task

Connecting a leader to spinnerbaits, hooks, swivels, snaps and split rings.

Knots and ratings

☆☆☆☆   Two and a half turn Clinch Knot—heavy mono

☆☆☆☆   Five turn Clinch Knot—light leaders

☆☆☆☆☆ Palomar Knot—spinnerbaits

☆☆☆☆   Double wrap Uni Knot—split rings

Comments

This group contains the best of the 'jam' knots. The two and a half turn clinch is a superior connection when using mono leaders from #50 to #100—and flexible coated wires. When using lighter leaders, the five turn clinch offers uncompromised security when properly seated.

Some fisherfolk insist on take an additional step—passing the tag end through the gap in the untightened knot where the tag end comes off the top of the coils to pass through the bottom loop. This step cants and actually weakens the knot.

If there's a single connection that delivers superior holding when tied in monofilaments to 30lb—and gel spuns—it's the Palomar Knot. The reasons aren't hard to fathom. The crossover is diagonal rather than at right angles. This spreads the load to create a less concentrated hot spot as pressures approach critical mass.

Split rings are frequently used as an attachment point for lures. They are optional where the tow point is fixed to the lure body, but where it is on the bib, a split ring is often used to keep the assembly in place. As much as anything, split rings are convenient solution but have a fatal chink. Under tension, thin and slippery gel spun easily works its way inside split rings and for that reason should never be directly attached. The safest way with mono and flexible coated wires is to form two wraps and secure with a three or four turn Uni Knot. Those steps provide a fair enough buffer against the sharp ends of wires in some rings.

PALOMAR KNOT

The Palomar knot provides a simple means of attaching hooks, either to the end of your line or trace, or along your line as is the case when rigging a drop-shot for soft plastics.

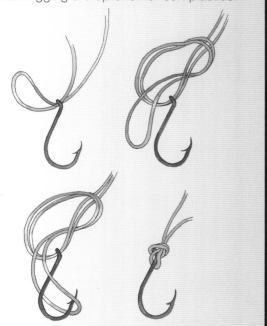

CLINCH KNOT

Clinch knots work best when attaching hook eyes and the like that have a similar or less diameter of the line being used. Thicker surfaces invite slippage and are better served with a Palomar or Uni knot. When using monofilaments under 20 kg breaking strain, make five turns. The two and a half turn version is ideal for heavier lines but needs to be carefully tightened. The so-called locked Clinch knot – where the bitter end forms a loop to the side of the wraps, through which is passes, can be a negative as it has a canting effect that works against proper tightening.

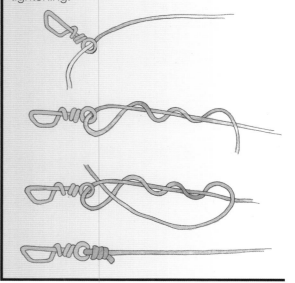

Task

Joining gel spuns, connecting top shots.

Knots and ratings

☆☆☆☆   Back to back Uni Knots

☆☆☆   Loop 2 Loop

Comments

When joining braids of equivalent diameter use a six/six mix. Where there is a disparity double the lighter. With mono to gel spun top shot joins are four/six, respectively. This provides security and a relatively small profile. If the mono underline isn't to be used in fights it's a good step to make this as light as possible. A lighter mono more evenly fills the spool core.

Deleting Doubles

For as long as most of us can remember, a double at the working end of the mainline has been the basis of any leader arrangement for lure and fly fishing—with the exception of freshwater situations to do with trout. Tied in mono, the bimini twist and Australian plait both deliver pretty close to 100 per cent knot strength. The rationale was, and still is, that anglers then had two strands with which to tie mainline leader connections and be able to retain the full tensile strength of the mainline. Things aren't the same for gel spuns. The bestest Bimini might yield 75 per cent. Might!

Old habits die hard, and in this gel spun age doubles formed with the time honoured bimini twist still flourish. Ditto alternatives like the Australian Plait, which gives

BACK TO BACK UNI KNOTS

The back to back Uni knot can be used to join lines of similar or different diameters.

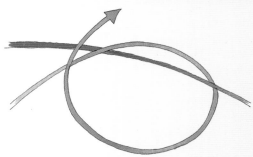

Step 1: Overlap the lines to be joined and encircle one line with the tag of the other.

Step 2: Wrap the double strand inside the loop formed.

Step 3: Four wraps are usually made.

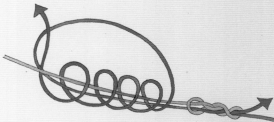

Step 4: Close the knot, but not too tightly, then do the same with the other length of line.

Step 5: Two knots are formed, one in each line, around the other.

Step 6: Slide the knots together, tighten each in turn, and trim the tags.

the best of all percentage breaks and for that reason has favour amongst an ultra light spin cadre. The quirks of gel spuns are such that the simplest of all, a six turn overhand knot—a kind of bastardised spider hitch and an abomination of a knot in monofilament—breaks on a par with the bestest Bimini.

All of which begs the question: is a double necessary?

Nah, there's absolutely no advantage to having one.

A double, in fact, can be a liability. Besides the time factor, not an inconsiderable matter for those with four thumbs, the inescapable consequence of any knot used to make a double is that what could be the weakest link in the chain is created right there. The knots and rigs explained elsewhere in this book more than compensate for deleting doubles. But there's no shortcutting the inflexible rule that with hard fishing, all knots and rigs needs regular inspections and replacement.

A Sticky End

The cyanoacrylate (CA) ester adhesives, variously known as super glues are not some magic formula. They might, however, offer peace of mind for the time being but no permanent bond. As a matter of course, all knots and joins, whether glued or not, should be replaced after a time, and sooner after heavy use.

Super glues have a limited application in immobilising knots in gel spuns. And while dissimilar molecular structures prevents any penetration a surface bond, albeit temporary, can be achieved by an initial application of an oxidising primer like Loctite 770. Generally speaking, CA glues are gap filling and saturate the air space within the knot, physically locking turns. Because of high shear strength, movement within the knot is, to a point, contained.

TAGS AND STUBS ·

For the purpose of this panel, those little bitter end bits of braid beyond a knot will be the tags. Stubs are a reference to similar monofilament ends on braid to mono connections. In the past, these little extras had no purpose and were closely trimmed. Braids have changed that trend. If for nothing else than peace of mind, given the indefinite slippage of knots in braids—until reaching a critical mass—some tag is better than none.

The fastidious who insist on trimming knots flush do themselves a disservice by continuing. The great insurance of having a few millimetres of tag is that the overhanging fibres unravel and catch, thus helping to arrest slippage. In mildly weedy water, the loose yarn will often snare those single strands that will otherwise ruin the presentation. Stubs, on the other hand, need to be trimmed flush. Moreso on braid to mono leader connections on casting rods. Fingernail clippers are a handy tool for that job.

Breakage rates on graphite composite rods have risen dramatically since the advent of braids. The most common cause is inflicting bends beyond 90 degrees while attempting to free snagged lures. To keep pace with the breakage rate, some makers offer very generous warranty provisions.

WORKING WITH WIRE

Connecting Braid or Mono to Single Strand Wire

Use pliers to double the wire and make a small turnover—much the same as a turned-in hook eye

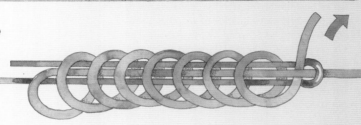

Mono to single strand wire

Insert the bitter end of the leader through the turndown and form a 7 turn snooze.

Secure the end under the leader material at the head of the knot.

Tighten and trim excess wire and leader

Braids to single strand wire

Same procedure as with mono – but double the braid and make twice as many (at least 12) wraps.

The Haywire Twist

This method is pretty much standard for attaching hooks and related hardware to non-pliable single strand wires and to create an end loop.

Step 1. Make a teardrop shape with the wire end, adjust the loop size and with the wires at 90 degrees to each other twist both simultaneously using thumb and forefinger. It is important that each strand is twisted evenly – not just one around the other.

Step 2. Repeat the process till four complete twists are made.

Step 3. Bend the bitter end so that it is at 90 degrees to the mainline axis.

Step 4. Make four tight and concentric wraps around the mainline.

Step 5. Form a small crank handle in the bitter end. Align it with the standing end and rotate in that direction. Properly done, the wire will break off flush. (old fencer's trick.)

Chapter SEVEN

A New Regime for Rigs

Were this chapter omitted, we'd still have Union Pacific and Cobb & Co., but not a lot that'd interest the likes of Jesse James or Ben Hall. Rigging and presentations—the loot—wouldn't have evolved to current levels were it not for gel spuns. That's not to say that there aren't hand-me-down rigs from grandpa's day. Oldies but goodies still have a place, but old dog fisherfolk reluctant to try new tricks risk being left behind as innovation and adaptation pick up pace.

Rarely does much time pass before the grapevine hums with word about something new. Little things mostly, that provide the package with more fish appeal while not compromising the security. This handful covers the main bases. And as anglers give more thought to what they're offering fish and the way they dish it up, there'll be more to come.

The innovation and adaptation goes much deeper than this dozen from my bag of tricks.

Offshore Bottom Rig

Rationale and Function

With gel spuns permitting offshore anglers to operate at depths not possible with monofilaments it makes sense to cover as many options as possible with rigs.

Braid or mono, fish or no fish, the trip up to the boat remains the same for terminal rigs. With that mindset, lead sinkers are replaced with a knife jig above which a soft plastic and cut bait combo has wide demersal fish appeal. Having the natural bait uppermost keeps it away from pickers and dovetails with the fact that when fish come off the bottom

to take a bait it's with the sort of rush that enhances the potential of a hookup. Alternately, the combo can be reversed, with, say, a tough natural bait like Octopus—or leg thereof—on the bottom hook and soft plastic above that.

Rigging

Suggest a rod length or so of 50lb mono leader for average deep sea tackle. This can be attached to the braid mainline with a Harro knot or slim beauty. A swivel can also be employed with uni knots both sides.

The knife jig or pirk employed in sinker role has an upper split ring that is attached to the leader with a uni knot. An assist hook (single or tandem) is fitted to the upper part of the jig using a girth hitch. The lower end of the jig is stripped of any hardware.

A metre or so above the jig a 'straight' hook (heavy worm type—O'Shaughnessy or Limerick—so long as there's no set or kirb) is attached (point uppermost) to the leader with a palomar knot. In this situation, a properly tied palomar knot will ensure that the hook will lay at right angles to the leader.

Add a second hook a metre or so above using the same procedure. A standard 'straight' hook is best used, rather than a dedicated worm type.

As mentioned above, the order of hooks and baits can be reversed to suit the situation.

Fishing

Best results happen where angler and / or boat provide movement. The lift provided by the swell can be sufficient when at anchor. In deeper water, jig weights need to be increased to compensate for current and drift. Some line management is needed to maintain contact with the bottom. A rod imparted lift and sink technique will do the job. The 'artificials' do not have to do much when 100 metres or more down. The simple fact of being there is enough. Triple headers are not uncommon when over schooling fish.

Spinnerbait Light

Rationale and Function

Angler opinion is heavily on the side of spinnerbaits being fitted with a stinger hook to boost the strike to hookup ratio. Of various touted arrangements, a smaller free swinging stinger seems in the minority but, in my experience at least, is a superior setup. Shielded by the skirting material, the free swinging stinger remains remarkably snag and weed proof yet is beautifully 'catching' with bass, goldens and greenfish.

Rigging

Any small to medium sized spinnerbait adapts. The Gamakatsu G-Stinger is light, sharp, very strong and easy to attach—a simple girth hitch over the main hook.

Jam knots are preferable when attaching spinnerbaits. Of a shortlist that includes the uni knot, clinch knots and the palomar knot, the latter offers superior strength when the spinnerbait is attached directly to the gel spun mainline. Most anglers prefer to use a mono leader—for peace of mind, as much as anything. This can be attached with back to back uni knots with leaders up to 30lb breaking strain,

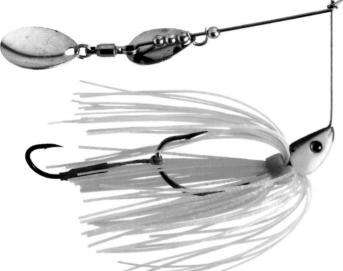

Fishing

Australian anglers have adopted the 'slow roll' Americanism to describe the main retrieve pattern and pace for spinnerbaits. Spinnerbaits also work in the vertical plane. Cod hit them as they flutter down to lairs. A 'helicopter' technique also works during pauses in the retrieve to adjust depth.

There are subtle speed variations available with different blade configurations. The spearhead shaped willow blades afford faster retrieves and are a good choice for prospecting bass on the open water reaches of impoundments. The more roundish Colorado and Indiana blades are best for the slower retrieves that expose the lure for longer in and around cover. Whatever the type, the G-Stinger addition is a very effective addition.

Spinnerbait Heavy
Rationale and Function

Weighty spinnerbaits are an Australian evolution aimed at Murray cod. Designed to run deeper, they are given bulk by the addition of a suitable soft plastic. Luremakers work on the greenfish territorial nature—the bigger the intruder, the more threat it poses.

Rigging

The stinger is wholly inserted midway along the soft plastic, leaving the gape and point exposed.

The main hook is then inserted into the head of the plastic and worked along so that the point passes through the eye of the stinger. The arrangement is 'fixed' with the addition of a small plastic disc located in the gape of the main hook.

The same jam knots used for light spinnerbaits apply. However, a leader is mandatory. Bare braids do not last long when in contact with the raspy greenfish jaws. A short length of 30–50lb mono is adequate.

This is joined to the mainline with the Harro knot or slim beauty.

Fishing

Cast to cover and a slow roll retrieve. Heavy spinnerbaits have also taken some mighty fish on the troll.

The Murray Cod is an Australian national treasure.

THE HELICOPTER TECHNIQUE - GETTING BIT ON THE DROP

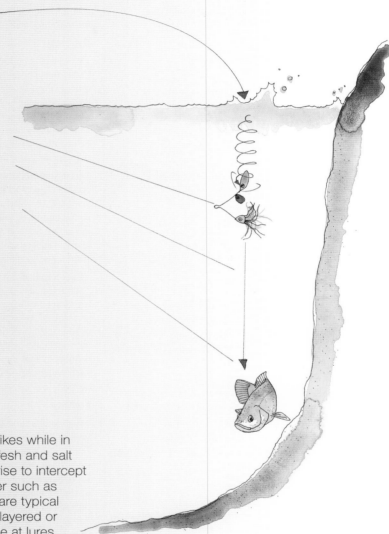

Make a high lob or flat trajectory cast according to the water. A higher cast allows the lure to sink more vertically against steep cover like rock walls. But requires a high rod tip that is lowered to maintain a tight line as the lure sinks. Open water does not require such an allowance.

Engage the reel the instant the lure makes a splashdown.

Reel in any slack line to maintain tension as the lure sink.

Note: When deep water jigging for demersal oceanic species, any tension from rod, reel and angler while the lure is going down will hamper the sink rate.

Sinking lures pick up bonus strikes while in free fall. They happen in both fresh and salt situations. Cover oriented fish rise to intercept lures as they sink. Vertical cover such as rockwalls and undercut banks are typical locations. School oriented fish layered or stacked in open water will swipe at lures falling through their midst. Anglers can capitalise on those situations by being ready.

So called on account of the blades of spinnerbaits auto-rotating during freefall, the helicopter technique is a much broader – and effective – way to score hookups prior to the retrieve getting underway. It is especially effective when addressing cover that has some vertical aspect – such as rock walls in lakes. Ambush feeder freshwater fish frequenting those places will rise to intercept lures as they fall.

Getting 'bit on the drop' as the fisho lingo goes, happens frequently in fresh and salt open waters with schooling fish. And with a wide range of sinking lures that include vibes, blades and pirks. The fishing method is to engage the reel the instant the lure hits the water and with the rod tip held low, progressively reel in slack so that the lure sinks on a tight line. When there's a take, strike with the rod – but don't forget to be cranking hard at the same time.

Integrated Paddletail Augmented

Rationale and Function

Paddletail soft plastics have become increasingly popular with fish that leap and shed hooks. Barramundi are a case in question. To adjust the odds, anglers have doctored the type with the addition of a treble.

Rigging

Custom made jigheads have an eyelet where a treble can be added. With integrated types, an effective method is to add a treble to a split ring, which in turn is added to a swivel. The swivel is then drawn up through the lure and looped over the rigid hook. Crimping will keep things in place.

A leader is advised, there are options already explained about connecting to the mainline with knots selected according to the leader thickness.

As a general rule of thumb, jighead / soft plastic combinations perform better when attached with a loop knot.

Fishing

Integrated paddletails are a highly versatile and effective soft plastics genre for working both in the vertical and horizontal. Options include a sink / twitch on the drop and a lift / twitch retrieve. A slow roll punctuated by pauses gets the best.

Paddletails

Rationale

Paddletail-type soft plastics combine realism with a retrieve envelope that can be dawdled down to the slowest speeds. They can be fished throughout the water column and in, through and over the dense weed and intimidating brush and snag cover.

Rigging

Paddletails include integrated varieties where the body material is moulded over the hook as well as unrigged types. Some integrated types come fitted to an underside treble. Those without can be doctored with a simple arrangement – a treble, split-ring, swivel chain. The swivel is drawn up through the underside of the soft body material and after being located over the hook is withdrawn back into the body material.

Bare paddletails are called swimbaits. They can be rigged on jigheads and on special hooks with weighted shanks – predictably called swimbait hooks. Some jigheads have provision for the addition of a treble hook. Trebles are a handy addition for snatch and grab feeders and leapers.

Paddletails are a second to none choice for attacking intimidating water. Integrated types can be weed/brush proofed by bridging the space between eyelet and hook point with a link cut from disused body material. Bare swimbaits can be likewise proofed with weighted or unweighted swimbait hooks.

Fishing

Paddletails lend themselves beautifully to a straight slow roll retrieve. Variations can include pauses that allow the lure to hover or sink according to weighting. The versatility of the format is underlined by the fact that it can be also be burned across dense surface vegetation and slowed for the pockets and edge. Twitches need to be kept to a minimum as they have a destabilising effect that eats up retrieve distance.

The Bendback Deceiver

Rationale and Function

The Bendback was once a specific fly pattern. Over the years it has evolved into a tying style. The same thing can be said of Lefty's Deceiver, saltwater's original swimming fly. Combine the two concepts and we have the most weed proof and snag resistant of all flies. In and around snags, sticky water and the salad weedbeds other patterns do not allow the same percentage of clean retrieves. The reversed hook that's the basis of the Bendback Deceiver offers an improved capacity to find its way through trouble spots. As for the hooking, there's no contest, alternatives such as weed guards can also be fish proof.

Rigging

Attach to the leader with a loop knot so as to maximise a freedom of movement.

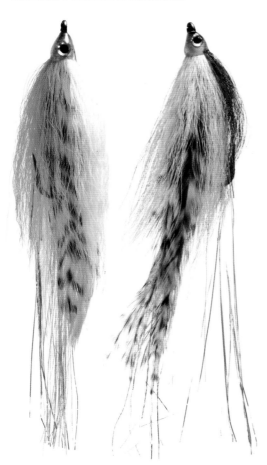

Fishing

Fished on a variety of line densities, the Bendback can address the water column.

An effective retrieve cadence is two quick strips followed by a pause. Retrieves can be adjusted to what might work on the day.

Mini Lures Rigged With Singles

Rationale and Function

It's a fishing fact of life that single hooks hold fish better than trebles.

In the case of mini lures, fitting singles of an appropriate gauge allows pro-active presentations in and around weedy areas. While singles will still snare weed strands, a sharp rip is often sufficient to sever the strand.

Rigging

Gamakatsu produce a 'Single Lure Hook' that has the eye parallel to the shank. They work best in slender minnow types with provision for a belly and rear hook. The belly hook is arranged point forwards and the tail hook, point upwards. A smaller tail hook is an option that has no downsides.

Where bass and other smooth mouthed fish are targeted, anglers can dispense with. leaders. The bare gel spun cuts through weed strands far more efficiently than mono. An effective way of directly attaching lures is with a 6 turn uni knot not fully

tightened, so as to leave a loop. This can be readjusted after each fight or, if it's a good fish, re-tied.

Fishing

A rip-pause-rip retrieve gets the best from mini lures thus modified. Baitfish-like lures that momentarily hang in weed strands then suddenly dart forward are ideally suited to situations where freshwater fish hunt weedy lake margins.

Descending Trebles

Rationale and Function

An increase in the running depths of three treble floating / diving lures can be achieved by retrofitting hooks in descending—no pun—order. The arrangement has the effect of creating and maintaining head-down attitude thus increasing the paravane effect of the bib.

Rigging

The set up I use is to change the 3 x #2 trebles typically supplied on suitable 120–150 mm lures. The retrofit consists of a #1 at the front, #2 in the middle and #4 in the tail.

The lures appropriate to this modification have bib and body mounted tow eyelets.

They come packaged with a split ring fitted to that eyelet. A small, strong, cross-lok snap is useful for lure changes but make sure it does not overhang the edge of the bib as leaping fish—which weight a lot more through their violent motion and without the support of the water—can distort the fitting and cause it to fail.

Leader setups as appropriate to the species and location.

Fishing

The depth increments are significant. Slow trolling for lake barramundi (the concept would also be ideal for striped bass and salmon in American lakes) with 100+ metres of #20 braid beyond the rod tip, a designated 7–8 metre capable lure can go deep enough to get the bends….over 40ft in some instances.

Dressed Rear Treble

Rationale and Function

There's nothing new to adding some sparkle to hooks. Some lure makers have been enhancing their lures this way for years. I'm a believer and use flash material (usually silver or pearl) to add twinkle to the rear treble in shallow diving minnows. The concept also works on weighted paddletails by adding the material immediately in front of the hook.

Rigging

Draw 10–15 strands of flash material—don't overdo it—through the eye of the treble and lash down with fly tying thread and lacquer. Trim the excess so that the material is very slightly longer than the treble.

Fishing

The concept performs best on lures that lend themselves to a twitch-pause-rip-pause retrieve.

Freddo the Flexible

Rationale and Function

Freshwater fish recognise frogs. Anglers have been acknowledging that for decades. In Australia the first recorded uses were frog shapes cut from car tyres in the 1930s and used to great effect on barramundi. Fake frogs have undergone considerable development in more recent years with the epicentre being the largemouth bass scene. However, following the visit of American bass pros to fish in some lake barramundi tournaments, Downunder uses have exploded.

As a successful topwater technique, the essence isn't so much the likeness to the real thing but the presentation style it allows across lily pads and weed mats—waters that limit lure selection.

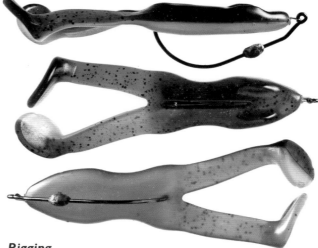

Rigging

The bulbous front end of fake frogs and the 'burn' retrieves that are a key to their success places a lot of strain on the anchor point at the hook eye. The Owner 'Twistlock Beast' is the superior hook for the job. As with all soft lures, it is imperative that the entire weight is borne by at hook eye. Any weight on the gape results in a wonky action.

Leader setups as appropriate to target species.

Fishing

In open water, the ideal 'frogging' action is to have water pushing over the front of the lure so as to create a significant bow wave, while simultaneously the feet are noisily splashing. Adjustments in rod angle will be necessary to maintain this strike-getting action throughout the retrieve.

When addressing topwater mats, a fast crank with pauses through the more open pockets can produce explosive strikes.

Suspend Minnow

Rationale and Function

There's no doubting the effectiveness of lures having negative buoyancy.

A suspend capability allows indefinite stalling in the strike zone or wherever appropriate during the retrieve. Dedicated 'suspend' lures are finely balanced and do not always perform as advertised. They are easily compromised by tinkering. Factory hook arrangements aren't always up to some fishing situations.

A way to get a partial suspend capability while not reducing the hook and hold function is to fine tune the leader and not the line.

Floating / diving minnow type lures tend to have a crisper action than types with a designated suspend capability—claimed or otherwise. The latter can be turned into lethal 'suspenders' (with attitude) by the addition of a length of lead core trolling line in the leader setup.

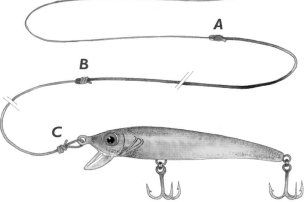

Rigging

Select a small bibbed shallow running minnow type. Trial and error will determine exactly how much lead core will be required. It will vary from lure to lure and, while castable, any more than a foot or so will create its own set of problems when being cast.

The knotting sequence is –

A. Braid to lead core: Harro knot

B. Lead core to mono leader: Albright knot

C. Mono leader to lure: Your favourite loop knot (Lefty's loop knot etc)

Fishing

The fishing system is a slow retrieve punctuated by pauses and slight twitches.

Spanish Swim Bait

Rationale and Function

This is a full fish bait for toothy gamefish like Spanish mackerel, wahoo, dogtooth tuna, barracuda and king mackerel. It also works a treat on billfish, big trevally, kingfish and amberjacks. It combines a lifelike swimming action with hooks and wire out of sight inside the bait

Rigging

Requirements

Any tuna, scad or similar round or deep baitfish from 300–600 mm in length.

2 x single strand wires, appropriate to the bait length, one a hook length shorter than the other.

One bomb type sinker (snapper lead)

Steps

1. Remove the top of the bait.

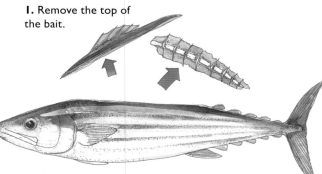

2. Cut out the backbone with scissors and remove.

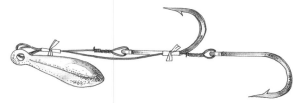

3. Have hooks pre-rigged on single strand wires. Their length needs to be so that the gape of the front hook is level with the eye of the secod hook.

Use a kitchen twisty to secure wires so that the hooks are opposed. The front hook rides upwards, the rear hook (which can be a size or two smaller) rides point downwards.

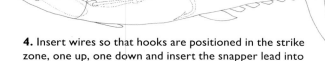

4. Insert wires so that hooks are positioned in the strike zone, one up, one down and insert the snapper lead into the mouth.

5. Align the snapper lead with the eyes of the haywire twists. Then through a central hole made through the head with a bait needle, insert a heavy mono leader making sure it passes through the snapper lead, both eyes of the haywire twists and out through the lower jaw.

Add a crimp and secure.

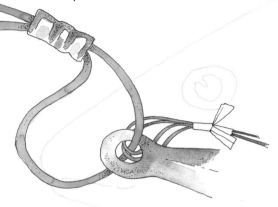

The running attitude and depth of this deadly bait can be varied. It will run deeper and have a tighter swimming action when the crimp is fixed immediately above the leader entrance hole. A shallower, more leisurely action is achieved with a larger loop with the crimp located in front of the jaw.

6. The final step is to close the surgery with thread and a bait needle and secure the jaw closed with a couple of stitches.

Fishing

Slow troll around the sides of offshore reef.

When toothy fish are the target, employ strike drag reel settings.

When other gamefish become involved, freespool and allow time for the bait to be swallowed before attempting to set hooks.

Bobbing Cray

Rationale and Function

This method of rigging dead crayfish in a lifelike and aggressive pose is a deadly rig in the world's freshwaters wherever these crustaceans are found.

Rigging

Add a metre or so of mono trace to the braid main line. Fit a ball sinker then attach a hook with a turned-in eye. Mustad's #540 'French' style is the hook for the job but may need sharpening.

Starting from under the tail, insert the hook so that it emerges where the tail meets the body. Twist the hook point 180 degrees and insert the point through the underside of the thorax so that it protrudes slightly through the upper body.

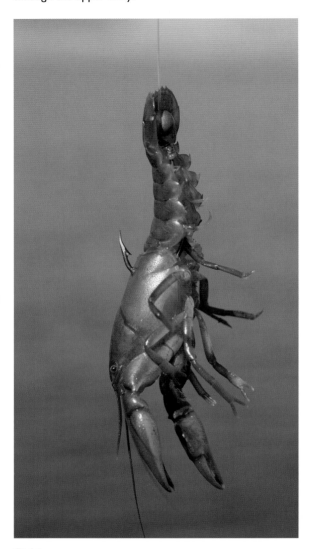

Fishing

Offering realism and notable snag proofing this rig is best fished over cover.

The best presentation is to free spool the crayfish to the bottom and work it in a yo-yo fashion. Besides the message of substance and scent, this mild up and down motion will cause the bait's claws to flare defensively... a sure strike trigger.

Whenever there's any resistance set the hook with a sharper upward lift... fish do not have hands.

Superglue'd Freshwater

Rationale and Function

A great idea when using natural baits in freshwater is rather than attempt inserting hooks—a messy operation that can distort things, simply glue the hook to the bait.

Rigging

Make sure both hook and bait surface are dry. Add a tiny droplet of cyanoacrylate glue. Popularly known as 'super glue', many brands of this strong and versatile adhesive are available.

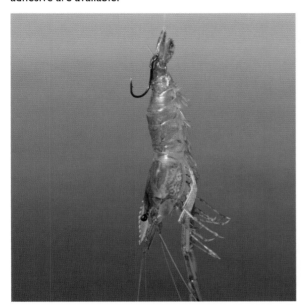

Presentations are more effective on the likes of trout when a light leader is used.

Fishing

The best presentation aspect is with the bait suspended. Bubble floats are ideal for stillwaters. Weightless presentations are effective in stream and lake but require ultra-light tackle.

Safety Pin Wire Rig

Rationale and Function

This is a quick and effective way to fish strip baits in offshore waters.

Rigging

Select a straight hook, connect with a single strand wire with a haywire twist extending the bitter end so as to make a half turn lock around the standing end.

Insert the bitter end through the upper part of a strip bait and re-engage.

Insert hook, skin side first, through the bait but ensure that the hook remains totally weight free.

The rig can be streamlined with the addition of a plastic squid.

Fishing

Can be trolled, cast or fished on the drift.

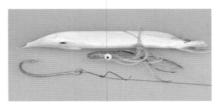

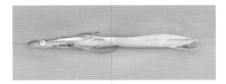

HOW TO SHARPEN A HOOK

Use a flat mill file and make a flat cut on the top of the point, opposite the barb.

Make sure the file strokes are away from the point, otherwise there's a risk of rolling the point.

This method produces a point with a spatula-like cross section - similar to needles used by surgeons.

This point configuration works from big game to mini tackle, and on jigheads especially.

A benefit often unseen is the way hooks thus sharpened will cut gristle and skin off the bone to gain an anchor point while minimising any tissue tear.

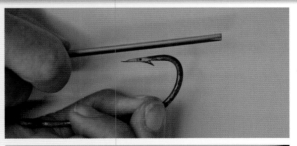

Chapter EIGHT

TAKE ME TO YOUR LEADERS

Leaders have two functions. The foremost is preventative. To protect the working end of the relatively vulnerable mainline from war zone conditions. The second, subterfuge; to disguise the presentation. There's many a situation where fish can be caught bareback on gel spuns. But few where overall results wouldn't have been better with the inclusion of a leader. In Australia, we're so conditioned to tying on leaders either to disguise or to protect presentations that few ever wonder why. But when researching trends through America's bass belt it was pretty obvious that the notion of a leader took some time to take root.

Beyond bass there are fish with teeth that cut like a scalpel. Others have raspy jaws and razor sharp spurs on gill covers, and leap when hooked—cutting instruments unsheathed and unleashed at Ali speed. In locations that include mangroves, jetties, wrecks, rapids, riprap and other rock-strewn water where gel spuns are in harm's way, leaders are mandatory.

Gel spuns can be somewhat obtrusive in the water. Their solid colours make them more visible than monofilaments. Although smaller cross-sections reduce visibility, fish in gin clear water are still able to detect their presence. That mere thought gnaws away at one's confidence. On crowded waters, fish seem to learn about lures, flies and even baits that have strings attached.

Material Choices

Leaders vary with the task. Materials include hard nylons, copolymers, flexible wires, fluorocarbon and heavy gel spuns. A single strand covers most mainstream uses. Depending on whether casting, trolling or waiting for a bite, and whether afloat or fishing by river, lake, estuary or ocean, lengths can extend from a foot to thirty. All things being equal, the chemical makeup of monofilament leader materials has a big impact on durability and withstanding scuffing but doesn't alter the importance of diameter.

Smoke and Mirrors

Some monofilaments are impregnated with silicone compounds. These reduce friction when the line comes in contact with a harder, more abrasive surface. But in the same sense that all car tyres wear, whether steel belt radial or retread, silicone additives leech and the line loses any advantage it may have possessed.

Much ado has been made of fluorocarbons, most of it focused on alleged invisibility. Amongst the Himalayas of opinion and comment printed on manufacturer packaging, in magazines and on the net, just a few foothills dwell on the fact that just the same as with other monofilaments, polyvinylidene fluoride (PVF) isn't a single entity. Various grades are manufactured, some containing chemicals that reduce costs but compromise the light refractive index. In the absence of advice from the marketers behind the many fluorocarbon brands, buyers are none the wiser and pay premium prices in the belief they're getting something fish do not see.

Developed 25 years ago by Korea's Kureha Corporation, PVF in a pure form has a refractive index of 1.33. Spring water comes in at 1.17 while the clearest monofilaments rate a 1.42. PVF is closer to that of spring water than clear nylons and copolymers.

The most objective tests have been those carried out by the long line fleets of Korea and Japan. Their vessels lay thousands of kilometres of line and a million baited hooks across and along the tuna and billfish migration routes. Yellowfin, big eye and bluefin tuna all have very large eyes and spend much time in the relatively well-lit ocean surface layers. Their vision capabilities rate amongst the best in the fish world and thus provided the

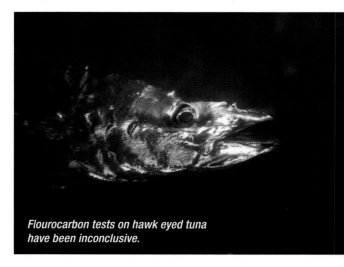

Flourocarbon tests on hawk eyed tuna have been inconclusive.

Only just. The leaderless get the odd break with toothy fish...sometimes

credentials as test bed species. When long line panels were hung with fluorocarbon droppers, both randomly and to a pattern, a trend that should have evolved didn't. While inconclusive, those results amounted, nevertheless, to a commercial thumbs down.

The misapprehensions also persist that fluorocarbons have better knot strengths or abrasion resistance than equivalent diameter nylons and copolymers. Neither is true. The molecules in polyvinyl fluoride cannot be as closely aligned as those in copolymers. Pound for pound, it's thicker, a fact that brings diameter into the equation.

Fluorocarbons do have an inalienable advantage in that being heavier than copolymers they offer a better sink rate. In some fly fishing situations, and finesse spinning with mini soft plastics, that virtue enhances presentations.

An inestimable 'feel good' factor seems to have won over hard fact in propaganda spread on behalf of fluorocarbons. Subjective to say the least, there are believers aplenty in flyfishing situations extending from New Zealand's gin clear rivers to Bahamas bonefish flats. Big Australian sales are racked up by competitive bass and bream anglers, convinced that there's a difference to be made in dingy water.

Fangs for Nothing

Wahoo, mackerels, bluefish (tailor) payara, barracuda, piranha, tigerfish, pike, musky, dogtooth tuna and sharks give rise to dental deliberations that'll require wire. There was a time when offshore anglers were taking a veritable plumber's shop to sea, such was the weight of wire, swages, and crimping tools needed to take on toothy fish. Wires included aircraft cable, Bowden cable, 49 strand, seven strand, various nylon coated wires that were a bit more malleable and single strand types, some of which could also be used to string the dingo fence.

The razor spur on the barramundi occasionally slices through the thickest mono leaders.

The Payara feeds on smaller fish that are impaled on a pair of snake like fangs.

The turn of the millennium has seen a dramatic shrinkage in wire use. The marlin charter fleet out of Cairns still swim rigged bait on 9 metre lengths of 0.29 galvanised wire. Sterner stuff remains in use amongst the diehard shark hunters being put out of business by the ban on taking the great white. Elsewhere, anglers have lightened up. The advent of new pliable alloys sees fishing wires being less obtrusive and more user friendly. TyGer Wire, an American made multi-strand type compatible with popular fishing knots and remarkably kink resistant, seems a peak development. It isn't cheap and is offered in black, nickel and copper coloured plastic coatings. Because of the extremely low friction coefficients of both materials, lots of wraps and careful tightening are required when joining wire to gel spuns.

Anglers tend to overdo wire. A little goes a long way. Despite a flexibility that allows anglers to use popular fishing knots, wires have a stiffening effect on the swimming actions of lures and flies. In offshore situations that I can relate to—fly fishing for Spanish mackerel, wahoo, dogtooth tuna and mako sharks—the twelve inches allowable in IGFA regulation leaders has been adequate.

The Tigerfish has one of the most intimidating mouths in the fish world.

Heavy gel spuns have growing support as leader material. It wears better than monofilaments of an equivalent diameter but is more visible. It has found favour as a shock leader with anglers casting big chuggers for giant trevally, the leader/main line connection has a softer passage through the guides. An annoying downside is the way the coarse surface of the material, and especially knots, attracts small pieces of weed and slime. The visibility that comes from a solid colour can also be off-putting. A downside of most wires is their stiffening influence on lure and fly actions. Less is better than more. A foot can be plenty.

Pre-Made Leaders

The perceived knotting complexities that have accompanied the up-take of gel spuns, along with a leader of some type becoming a mandatory addition, has seen a surge in the use of pre-made leaders. The availability includes commercially made nylon and fluorocarbon wind-ons fitted with a Dacron or hollow gel spun loop, short flexible wire rigged with swivel and snap, and a home made twisted variety based on a concept introduced by the Knotted Dog series.

Machine and hand twisted multi-strand leaders have enjoyed some popularity amongst barramundi anglers. The concept behind the much copied originals was to provide some cushion at the terminal end that would compensate for the lack of stretch in gel spuns. Twisted leaders have a major drawback in being somewhat bulky and thus visible.

Single strand wind-on leaders have a big following. Their main virtue is a trouble free passage through the rod guides when cast. This comes about through the extremely low profile of the loop to loop connection, between the gel spun mainline and a short Dacron intermediary. In more recent times, special 'hollow' gel spuns are being used for this purpose. Whatever the material, it acts on the finger trap principle after several centimetres of the leader is inserted and the end secured with fly-tying thread or a seven turn nail knot tied in 10lb mono. Winds-ons are commercially available, though many specialist anglers make their own.

Wind-ons are rightly advocated for deep jigging for amberjack, cobia, yellowtail kingfish, samson fish, cod and hapuku, and when casting big chuggers for giant trevally, trolling and live baiting for billfish. Of course, some knots are unavoidable, and when monofilaments get into the 100lb to 500lb range used for marlin, crimping systems become a more compact alternative.

Too Much or Not Enough?

Though pretty much predetermined by popular trends, important considerations are behind the choice of leader materials and lengths.

Firstly, the mouth and head structures of target species. Whether rubbery lipped, rasp jawed, toothy or not, smooth gilled or equipped with cutting edges, where danger zones are confined to mouths and gill covers, a foot or so bare minimum offers adequate protection—and great convenience—in intensive cast situations. Unnecessarily long leaders have a quelling impact on mild to medium action lures. Some allowance needs to be made for spiny bodies and tail scuta, though in my experience the dangers there seem more perceived than real. There's nothing perceived about rock, reef, riprap, line shredding pylons and other tidal structures. Amongst those terrains, gel spuns are more vulnerable than monofilaments of similar breaking strain.

Leader lengths are everything. They are limited by the rules of organisations like the IGFA, under which auspices many fish, otherwise there's nothing arbitrary. Generous safety margins are off-putting where subterfuge is needed—but for roughhouse all-in brawls with fish that do not ask questions, a bit more beats not enough.

When it comes to abrasion resistance and pliability, modern copolymers are taking over from the type 6 nylons. Mason and Schneider are popular brands amongst the latter.

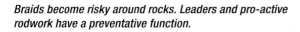

Braids become risky around rocks. Leaders and pro-active rodwork have a preventative function.

Soft Options and Hard Choices

Copolymers of various brand and origin are packaged and marketed as leader material. They offer what may be termed two lines in one—a toughened, annealed outer surface and softer, pliable inner core. Copolymers are a good choice for offshore and deep sea situations and along with clear, non-glint and pliable nylons they are a popular—and wise—choice for clean fighting, smooth skinned species with rubbery mouths and those containing small, non-meshing teeth that generally occupy open water habitat. Trout, salmon, bonefish, carp, zander are representative.

Ditto open water and cover oriented species with non-abrasive mouths but spiny bodies include various basses and perch, grunters, croakers, carangid clan trevally, tuna, kahawai, flathead, giant herring (lady fish),

Lake living browns require stealth and fine leaders.

queenfish, emperors and sweetlips, groupers, mulloway, drum, weakfish and many others.

Barramundi and tarpon are special cases. Both possess powerful underslung jaws that have the texture of coarse sandpaper. Poontangle and barrabusting are spectacular pursuits that are hard on leaders. The main damage happens during head shaking leaps. Within their natural element, water supports the weight of fish and places limits on the speed of movements. Those dynamics alter considerably as new stresses are introduced once fish are in the air, mouths open and gills flared.

A related dynamic that saves fish is to lower the rod to create slack whenever a fish leaps. Big tarpon call for heavier leaders than barramundi by virtue of their greater weight. Although more difficult to knot than a copolymer, a hard nylon is a better defence. The last time we fished the Florida Keys my flies, and the soft plastics of my fishing mate Jannine Saunders, were initially attached to 100lb mono—the accepted standard bite tippet size for tarpon. A hundred eyes watched some presentations. Nothing made a move. It wasn't until we went down to a clear, non-glint 60lb hard wearing nylon that we were able to get takes from individuals travelling with those passing schools. Trouble then was leaders being chaffed through before the fight was over. We'd had the best of it though, the acrobatics and furious charges. The latter half of tarpon fights are slugfests from which hundred pound, hundred year old fish do not always recover.

Tarpon have the most abrasive jaws of any non-toothed fish and require mono leaders that are heavy but not obtrusive.

Barramundi run a close second to Tarpon when it comes to the chafe effect of raspy jaws. The popular choice in leaders is a 50lb hard nylon – but at times that's not enough.

QUIRKY CHARACTERISTIC

A quirky characteristic lays in fluorocarbon to monofilament connections. Dissimilarity in the surface friction coefficients of both materials can cause the fluorocarbon to slip and the knot fail. That possibility increases with time and use.

Neither do fluorocarbons perform well when there are rapid increases and decreases in tension. Users can see this failing at work in snatch tests. The overriding consideration is to take extra care when forming and tightening fluorocarbon to mono connections and to change them regularly.

Chapter NINE

SPORTFISHING HORIZONS

The compelling advantages of gel spuns stem from diameter and stretch a fraction of that of monofilaments having equivalent breaking strain. Anglers are casting further, fishing deeper, hooking more fish and ending fights sooner.

Gel spuns deliver the message like never before. A rip or twitch with the rod tip can cause the lure to suddenly spurt, deviate or seductively shake, quiver and stall. Every inch of movement from the rod tip equates to an inch of movement from the lure. That sort of body language acts as a response trigger to predatory fish that may be watching or following. Crisper actions and deeper running depths are bonus consequences.

There's no better example than in the workings of the humble white bucktail jig—the most versatile single lure of all time and no accident to find packed amongst the survival gear for military personnel. Deadlier still is a technique for addressing the water column with jighead/soft plastic combinations. In skilled hands, the direct contact of gel spuns takes a tantalising 'bounce on the rod tip' retrieve to new heights.

Soft lures would have unfulfilled potential were it not for the intimate touch gel spuns provide. Techniques for fishing those squirmy flimflams and associate potions are closer to fishing with natural baits than bona fide cast and retrieve. Fish reactions tend to be less than the full-blooded strikes with which they hit a hardbody lure. With monofilaments the bite detection wasn't there to monitor all of those taps, mouthings and pick-ups. Anglers struck on suspicion. Now we can be certain whether a bump came from something inanimate or swimming.

Gel spuns are an end of days for drama queen hook sets. No more sweeping "sock it to 'em", just a gentle snap of the wrist—and a sharp hook. I'm not sure how welcome that advice would be amongst the tele-angler blokes who dress up like racing car drivers to go fishing and have boats almost as fast. On the box, bass are overdone. Viewers are conditioned to action—and commercial breaks. So when a fish doesn't perform, and it's hard to expect a lot from the average largemouth, then I guess the angler has to, covering himself in advance with anti-climatic hookup antics.

The majority of fish are hooked and battled at ranges comparable to those in bat and ball games. Pitchers and bowlers do their best to bamboozle batters by mixing deliveries and being unpredictable, but once the ball departs, that's it. Anglers have the luxury of staying in

Big league flyrod fish such as Striped Marlin have become much more achievable through the increased backing capacities braids offer.

control throughout. Retrieves can be paced slow, fast or a bit of both, whether a staggered, staccato path or something more akin to a Volvo being taken for a test drive by a 90 year old. Those things are entirely in their hands. Once beyond the transition from mono, events advance to where it isn't a just a matter any more of getting a good feel through the rod, but learning pro-active presentations—and how to quickly get the head of fish that wants to argue the toss.

Gel spuns enhance immeasurably those situations that, for various reasons, see anglers working at longer ranges. It may be a clear, shallow lake full of harassed fish or a school of breaking, boat-shy tuna. Gel spuns allow anglers to launch casts from distances where the boat is not an intrusive factor.

The Jigs Up

The vertical dimension opened up by superlines has spawned an entirely new range of tackle, the best of it hellishly expensive. Japanese design and manufacture leads the way. Japan has a class of travel oriented anglers who travel by the plane load in search of fish that challenge their manhood.

Surrounded by three oceans and with blondes aplenty, Australia is a popular destination. Quite apart from the *Caranx* clan, headed up by the giant trevally, there's the bruise brothers, the *Seriola* gang. This trio comprises the yellowtail kingfish—aka California yellowtail—amberjack and samson fish. All can grow to a hundred pounds. Offshore reefs and wrecks down to 200 metres are where some of the biggest fish are to be had.

Charter operations built around those line burners work out of ports on the Pacific, Southern and Indian Ocean seaboards. These are heavily patronised by visiting Japanese anglers, outfitted to the teeth and spooled up with 50/80 pound gel spun braids having a depth colour coding much the same as that used in

Called Kingfish in Australia and New Zealand, the Pacific Yellowtail is also found across the Northern Pacific from Japan to California

The aptly named Samson Fish is found on deep reef around the southern Australian coastline, growing to at least 100 pounds.

A Nicola Zingrelli image of a colourful Mediterranean Groper deep jigged in the Straits of Gibralta by a Japanese angler

The Red Bass is a found through tropical inshore seas of the Indo-Pacific. A close relative, the Cubera Snapper, occupies a similar niche in the Atlantic.

lead core trolling lines. The slimline knife jigs being produced in a dazzling array of reflective colours work at extraordinary depths. Hookups at 100 fathoms occur on some flat days. Making a jig do its thing that far down can demand a lot of angler effort. A technique that comes with experience is to time upwards movement of the jig with the rise of the boat with ocean swells. The additional kick is a sure-fire trigger.

In filling the deep jig niche, some very specialised tackle has been developed. Rods are between five and seven feet, have beer bottle tapers and extended grips. Because of a leverage advantage, long grips and hand holds higher than normal on the rod tend to covey the impression that the rod is pumping out more pressure than it actually is. The immutable fact is that the blank material anywhere below where a firm grip is taken during a fight becomes neutralised.

The bends thus inflected require a special construction. Hoop strength is provided by a scrim—graphite fibre spiral wrapped along the mandrel prior to baking. A full scrim adds too much wall thickness and weight for the blank to have any real casting function, but for those intense up/down stoushes that go with levering strong fish up from deep reef, there's nothing better.

Some Japanese jig rods sell for two grand. With design reflecting the task, these are built on specially made high carbon content blanks that have a high leverage, heavy lift capacity. Long foregrips, some ridiculously so, lessen the load on anglers while providing the impression that maximum heat remains on the fish. Big handles are a feature on a new wave of jig reels specifically designed and built for the stresses of the #50 and #80 gel spuns popularly used. Daiwa, Shimano and others offer jig reels in spin and overhead formats.

The bottom-bombers, as offshore bait fishermen are called down in the south seas, are able to fish even deeper, thanks to gel spuns. There's a double bonus there given the prohibitive price of lead these days, fuelled by sky high demands as a shielding material for nuclear power stations. As fishing depths increase, demersal fish get bigger and are more inclined to slam-dunk than nibble. Given the yardage involved, knockabout gel spuns that are braided from a heavier yarn have become a popular and cost effective choice.

The fractional differences in the diameter of gel spuns have an infinitesimal impact on fishing depths. In any case, the influences of current, tide, wind and drift on gel spuns are slight compared with their ballooning effect on monofilaments.

Bluewater Topwater

Mother ship charters to remote atolls have opened up a new chapter in sportfishing annals.

Anglers taking those cruises are able to explore the outer limits—theirs and those of their tackle. A 'Pacific Fleet' operates out of San Diego and ranges down to Clipperton Reef and other exotic locations. Initially there was some resistance to braids but as the compelling advantages that went with vastly increased line capacities for stand-up anglers already burdened with bulky reels, pragmatism prevailed. Anglers fishing mono can't be found along today's hot rails.

Notable amongst other long range operations scattered through the Pacific basin, is the fly-in service of Nomad Charters. Based in Hervey Bay, midway along Australia's east coast, the Nomad mother ships are anchored for weeks at a time at locations on the lower and outer Great Barrier Reef. Clients arrive via amphibious aircraft with reels brim full of #50 / #80 braids. Departing flights tend not be as heavily loaded.

To accommodate tight baggage limitations, the Nomad crew have developed heavy duty stick baits that are provided to clients from a mother ship stash. These are more aerodynamic than the coke can diameter chuggers that started the GT 'Samurai of the Sea' thing. And, a lot less elbow grease on the magnum casting tackle.

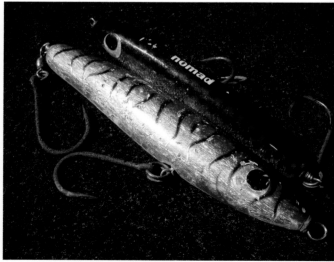

Nomad's explosive Oceanic Stickbaits.

Opah live in Pacific depths and for the first time lies within reach of anglers fishing big reels and braids.

A Fly over the Target

Braids have pushed flyfishing's bluewater boundaries by effectively doubling the backing capacities of reels. Salmon reels become sailfish capable. The hundred pound tuna barrier would remain unbroken were we still back in Dacron days. Nowadays the record Atlantic Bluefin is just short of two hundred. Marathon encounters with blue marlin wouldn't go the distance. Unlike other billfish—which sometimes make mistakes—blues do not open windows of opportunity for a quick tag or gaff shot. That reason, along with size and speed makes them the toughest of all opponents for big league flyrodders.

Tom Evans in good form. Dropping the rod when fish leap creates slack and eases the strain on hook anchor points.

The Longtail Tuna or Oriental Bonito is noted for long runs... and changes of direction when some distance from the boat. Anglers spooled with mono and dacron often were run out of line.

Valley of the Pings and the River Rambo

A couple of situations have been more graveyard for gel spuns than good news. The most notable is Egypt's Lake Nasser. Held back by the Aswan High Dam, this massive structure has created a lake on the upper Nile that's over 300 miles in length. The Valley of the Kings, tombs of the Pharaohs of antiquity, lay beneath its jade waters. A hundred thousand toiling labourers once hand cut sandstone and basalt blocks for the pyramids from bluffs overlooking the river. The crenellated outlines and chisel marks are still visible. One only has to be standing there in 120°F heat to get an inkling of what it would have been like. I'm an habitual barefooter and have been that way since a boy. It was too much for me.

A Nile Perch from jade waters now covering Pharoah tombs.

Our 'mother ship' and tender flotilla had stopped off for lunch in a quiet cove that first day en route to another location where we'd fish later in the afternoon and camp the night on warm Sahara sands. I couldn't wait—and after wolfing down a mysterious Egyptian nosh and a beer that tasted like it had been brewed in a sarcophagus—made my way to a nearby rock platform a rod length or so above water level.

On about the forth or fifth cast the one ounce Cordell Rattle Spot had just touched bottom after a thirty second sink. I'd commenced a staggered draw and sink retrieve and had barely got the cadence underway when the rod tip was reefed down by a hefty strike. Then nothing. Hastily re-rigging the braid on my baitcaster, I tied on a spare lure that'd dangerously been left to its own devices in my pocket. The cast was a duplicate of the previous. The hit happened on the drop. The five second hookup ended just as abruptly... ping, hero to zero, as they say. Loaded up with the latest superlines I'd gone fishing in a cradle of kryptonite. It was a long trip. I'd have traded a pallet of cold beer—Australian beer—for a spool of mono.

New Guinea is land of mountains, mystery and steamy ongo-bongo rivers hemmed in by walls of giant jungle hardwoods. It is a final frontier where heir and anthropologist Rockefeller vanished and where anglers armed with casting tackle battled big and enormously powerful freshwater snappers long before the ichthyology community became aware of their existence. Pound for pound, they are the world's toughest fish.

Close relatives of the cubera snapper of the Americas, they are classic ambush feeders, laying amongst log cover and intercepting prey in a lightning burst—but not before outflanking the intruder and snatching it in a thunderous direct line back to it's lair.

This introduces kinetics into the equation not found in any other fishing. Braided lines part with a pistol shot sound. Hard to conceptualise, but some lines (mono, Dacron and gel spuns) have snapped at spool zero from the sheer force, speed and friction of line dig.

The differences between Lutjanus goldiei and Lutjanus fuscens are obvious

The legendary Papuan Black Bass, pound for pound the toughest.

FINESSE

Monofilaments have always imposed limitations on ultra light sportfishing. All too often, the finest practical monofilaments (0.5–1.0 kg breaking strain) haven't been enough. The availability of gel spuns that offer breaking strains in the 2–4 kg range has taken finesse fishing to new levels of finery. Presentations not possible with the lightest practical monofilaments have opened a new and exciting world of micro jigs and mini lures. These include softs that blur the gap once existing between artificial lures and natural bait and hardbody vibes so realistic that fish will strike while the lure sits innately on the bottom. Within these scaled down scenarios, a hotrod mullet becomes a veritable marlin.

A pertinent associate demographic lies in the fact that many finesse fishing opportunities lay close to population centres. Whereas exotic species and trophy fish generally involve travel to locations that can be remote and faraway, much entertaining and exacting sportfishing lies at our back door. A door that would not have opened was it not for gel spuns.

A stud Spot-Tail Bass taken in a New Britain rainforest river.

Lutjanus goldiei, as it is more formally known, grows to unstoppable proportions. By the time the message flashes to the brain one's tackle is overloaded, the skiff is slewed and the fish in the sticks. In years of trying to counter their hit and run tactics and stupendous strength, tackle based on the snatch strap principle used on bogged vehicles, became a part answer. This involved rods with a scrim for lots of hoop strength, large baitcast reels with drags done up with pliers and the stretchiest 50lb mono one could find.

Named from the Goldi River near Port Moresby and also known as the Papuan black bass and Niugini bass, it has a distribution through the tropical archipelago of the Indo-Pacific region. The spot-tail bass is a close relative I named for obvious reasons after being taken to rivers (where blacks and spots live side by side) in New Britain by ex-pat Aussies on that beautiful island. It too grows big and fights hard, however anglers fishing (with braid) the smaller and clearer New Britain waters face neither the hazards nor fish sizes to be found in mother lode rivers of the Gulf of Papua.

To stray off-topic and sign off on Rockefeller, according to Leonard Nimoy, hosting an unsolved mysteries television series, Rockefeller was last seen clinging to an overturned canoe in a croc infested river mouth. Someone was pulling Spock's leg.

Rockefeller was last active in what is now the Indonesian province of West Irian. Following Japan's surrender in 1945, the Dutch resumed their colonial occupation of the archipelago known as the East Indies. Those territories included West Irian, the western half of the resource rich island of New Guinea. The eastern half would remain under the control of Australia for a few more decades.

Unlike the French in Vietnam, the Dutch were smart enough to realise it was time to cut losses rather than maintain an army of occupation in the face of growing unrest. The Dutch had pacified a region along the Digul River where a tribe known as the Asmat had been warring with neighbours for centuries, Rockefeller was studying those head-hunters and had them re-enact a raid. But things got out of hand and arrows flew.

Freshwater Thumbnails

If you excuse the butchered French, transcendence of angling might be reflected in the axiom that one person's fish is another person's poisson.

Take carp, perhaps the most universal of fish, on every continent except Antarctica. A six pounder from a Parisian sidewalk by the Seine is a pedestrian stopper. Carp are finned deities in Japan, worshipped rather than tempted with some forbidden bait. They're fishy business in the UK, big fishy business, where a Tess the twenty or Gerty the thirty is a ticket to piscatorial paradise. In Australia, they're shot on sight. A declared noxious species that do much eco-harm to river and lake habitat, stockmen and sporting shooters often partake pot-shots at cruising fish in outback rivers.

A trophy Carp taken in the shadow of a castle in Spain.

Carp are a multi-species amongst with *Cyprinus carpio* is the most widespread.

It sometimes reaches 25 kg—about half the size of the mahseer, the biggest branch on the family tree. Mahseer are found on the Indian subcontinent, notably in the Cauvery River where the prime bait is a concoction of dough impregnated with the sap of a local tree. Carp are polymorphic in the extreme. The aquarium trade produces grotesque mutations.

Catfish of various kinds are also to be found in freshwaters from the sub-arctic to the tropical. The vundu, found in Africa, and subari from South America— along with a European species—are amongst those achieving crocodilian proportions.

Originally from Europe, brown trout have done well in the Antipodes. Some of the biggest are sea run fish in Patagonia where the wind never rests. New Zealand's rivers are justifiably world famous while Tasmania has a unique stillwaters fishery.

Salmon runs in the Northern Hemisphere aren't quite the legend of yesteryear, though Alaska is still a place to fish till one's arms drop. There's argument as to what's biggest, the king salmon of the northern Pacific rim or mouse eating Taimen found in Mongolia. Both are said

Catfish of various clans grow to huge sizes in worldwide tropical and temperate freshwaters.

Col Davis Stephenson (US Army ret.) with a nice Dorado taken in the Parana River, Paraguay.

to reach 100 pounds. Salmon have been transplanted to the sea seas with mixed results. A thriving quinnat (king) fishery was established in rivers like the Rakaia, Rangitatta and Waitaki but was killed by the official mis-management of commercial netting in river mouths and too many salmon farms. Tasmania has developed a lucrative Atlantic salmon fishery based on raising penned fish. These enclosures are under constant attack from seals. Anglers delight in the thousands that sometimes escape fro ripped pens.

In appearance and habit, dorado aren't unlike salmon. The name however, the Spanish word for gold, is an apt description. Dorado are found in major South American rivers. The mother lode is in the Parana River, water shared by

Chuck Yeager and Gary Loomis (both front kneeling) and the GLoomis crew with a catch of King Salmon

As Honcho at Swedish reel maker ABU, CO Eriksson spent years as a globetrotting fishing goodwill ambassador. This Chaffalote is a kind of Payara from Paraguay's Parana River.

It might be argued that the Tigerfish gets the name as much from the body stripes as the teeth. The species is widely distributed through African rivers and lakes.

Argentina, Paraguay and Brazil and where large scale migrations occur. The massive Itaipu Dam disrupts these movements but has created a tail race fishery of international renown, known as La Zona it is limited by the Argentine authorities to five boats at any one time.

The spectacular payara reaches 20 kg, likes fast water and leaps. Instantly recognisable through a pair of sabre like teeth that recess in upper jaw holes, the Payara is found in South American rivers from the Orinoco to the Parana. Venezuela is the place, but alas, no place for the gringo.

If a show of fangs is anything to go by, the Tigerfish has the meanest mouthful. This African sportfish is variously found from Lake Nasser on the Nile to the Okavango Delta in Botswana where there is a well oiled tourism infrastructure. Great fishing was to be had in Zimbabwe—but that was prior to despot dictator Mugabe going mad; he must die soon. The largest sub-species, the goliath tigerfish, reaches 50+ kg but seems restricted to the Congo River, an even more dangerous place for a white man armed with just a fishing rod. Tigerfish have been proclaimed as the world's most dynamically powerful freshwater fish… they're certainly Africa's.

Nile Perch this size are an uncommon catch as unregulated commercial fishing escalates in African lakes.

The Nile perch is the largest of what can be described as the world's great freshwater gamefish. Reports of gargantuan specimens outweighing a trio of regimental blacksmiths may be the result of too many gins at the officers' club back in colonial days. Fish in the order of 300 pounds have been captured in African lakes as far flung as Chad, Turkanka, Nasser and Victoria. Massive overfishing has decimated stocks and a once common hundred pounder is now a fish of a lifetime. There's bitter irony in the fact that the voracious Nile perch was introduced into Lake Victoria, the world's largest freshwater lake, shared by nations with patrol boat navies. The impact on smaller fish in the food chain has been devastating. These once provided subsistence fishing to villagers living around the lake. The Nile perch is thus contributing to its own demise in that water. Starving millions could end up with even less.

Barramundi are a dynamic fish with a distribution from Hervey Bay, midway along Australia's east coast through various Indo-Pacific archipelagos to Sri Lanka and beyond. Unlike close relative the Nile perch, it cannot breed in dams. However fish stocked into stillwaters are commonly attaining sizes not usually encountered in the wild. Those lakes contain incalculable bait fish biomasses that have formed self-perpetuating populations. Lake living barramundi eat more and expend less energy in the hunt for food. In time they will surpass—if not already—the Nile perch as the world's largest available stillwaters gamefish.

Few fish are more deeply etched into the fabric of the nation's folklore than the Murray cod. The size, aggressive nature and loose feeding habits of these mottled national treasures is the stuff of legend. It

A howl of delight from skilled angler Stu Wilson at his first Barra... and a Barra career that might be all downhill.

Amongst the less tangible impacts of braids has been a catch and release ethic being applied to national treasures like Australia's Murray Cod.

is a fish that spans generations. From times of the Murrumbidgee whalers, hard, mustachio'd men with whipcord bodies—so named after the boats they'd row in pursuit of river giants. Double-enders of Moby Dick design, clinker built from spotted gum planks—to today's fast lane hulls that travel faster than the family car.

When I first started fishing in Papua New Guinea the authoritative textbook of the day, Munro's Fishes of New Guinea, made no mention of giant freshwater snappers. There was nothing to go by save for a couple of magazine articles by speculative writers. The two had common threads. The fish was a *Lutjanid* of some kind, but exactly what, no one knew. And it pulled like blazes; like nothing they'd previously hooked—and they fished a lot. So I went. On spec.

Sniffer dogs weren't part of the customs rigmarole at airports, otherwise I'd have been busted. My smuggled specimen was delivered to John Paxton, Curator of Fishes at the Australian Museum. A couple of weeks later a call came through from the obliging ichthyologist with the American accent. He'd rummaged around in a back room and located a match. *Lutjanus goldiei* had been collect from the Goldie River out from Port Moresby by an Australian naturalist named Macleay sometime in the late 1800s.

It was obviously a member of the worldwide *Lutjanidae* family but Macleay's was of a size that saw it lumped in with the sundry palm sized of the clan. Dr. Paxton expressed surprise at my assertion that it grew to goodness knows how big and that a couple of hooked fish had nearly pulled me out of the boat.

Embolden by those events I followed it to the island of New Britain where the fisho grapevine had it that another 'big bass' as they were called lived in the rivers there. Just as large as *goldiei* and immensely powerful, it seemed to live in pure freshwater. I called it the spot-tail (bass), a name that's stuck. The tail blotch is a characteristic shared by some *Lutjanids*. Existing scientific data from the Philippines had already identified the species as *Lutjanus fuscens*.

By the yardstick of a kilogram of fish per kilogram of line breaking strain, the brute strength, habitat and lightning rush striking fish make back to their log strewn lair, a tougher fish won't be found than *Lutjanus goldiei*. The spot-tail runs a close second. I'm not alone in those opinions.

FRESHWATER HEAVYWEIGHT RANKINGS

FISH	SIZE	ACCESS	WILLINGNESS TO BITE	BAIT	LURE	FLY	FIGHT
Carp	★★★	★★★★★	★★★★	★★★★★	★★	★★★	★★★
Catfish	★★★★★	★★★★★	★★★★★	★★★★★	★★	★★	★★★
Trout	★★	★★★★	★★★	★★	★★★	★★★★★	★★★
Salmon	★★★	★★★★	★★★	★★★	★★★★	★★★	★★★
Dorado	★★★	★★★	★★★	★★★★	★★★★	★★★	★★★★
Payara	★★★	★	★★★	★	★★★★	★★★	★★★★
Tigerfish	★★	★★★	★★★	★★★	★★★★	★★★	★★★★
Nile Perch	★★★★★	★★★	★★★★	★★★★	★★★★	★★★	★★★
Barramundi	★★★★	★★★★★	★★★★	★★★★	★★★★★	★★★★	★★★★
Murray Cod	★★★★	★★★	★★★	★★★★	★★★★	★★	★★★
Niugini Bass	★★★★	★★	★★★★	★★★★	★★★★	★★★★	★★★★★
Spottail Bass	★★★★	★★	★★★★	★★	★★★★	★★★★	★★★★★

Chapter TEN

STICK IT TO 'EM

Gel spuns are doing to monofilaments what gunpowder did to bows and arrows, and more recently the way graphite composites went about sealing the fibreglass blanks' coffin. Greenhearts to graphites, animal gut to gel spuns, the developmental trails of rods and lines ran in parallel. The evolution of rods is rich in history—ancient, medieval and modern. The times of Isaac Walton saw 'greenheart' rods hewn from the same elastic English yew sapwood used for the legendary longbow. Caber-like compared with today's lightweight composites, greenheart rods soldiered on into the 20th Century.

As the age of Britannia opened trade routes to The Orient, bamboo became a better rod material. English and Scottish craftsmen began building salmon and trout flyfishing rods for peerage and other products of the British class system. The work was exacting and time consuming. Tapered triangular strips were cut from lengths of bamboo, six in all, forming a hexagonal cross section when glued. Flyfishing folklore has it that bamboo staffs from the outer parts of the stand were favoured. The reasoning was that being more exposed to the full force of hurricanes in the South China Seas they were a bendier bamboo. The multi-piece make up of split cane rods was a reflection on the presence of a node every foot or so along a prime staff. Split cane fly rods were priced beyond the means of the working people of the day. Whether through design or happenstance, a prohibitive pricing regime persisted with fly rods for over a century.

In the immediate years following World War II, the manufacturing priorities in developed countries didn't include sporting equipment. Not to be deterred, some strong arm'd Americans converted whippy tank aerials into fishing poles. A huge war surplus saw a ready supply.

Within the decade solid fibreglass emerged as a rod material. Technology had worked out that by melting glass and allowing the liquefied material to be drawn through minute holes while still hot, flexible filaments with high tensile strength could be produced. These could be arranged longitudinally, tapered and treated with a bonding resin.

A major breakthrough came in the form of fibreglass cloths that could be rolled onto a mandrel and baked in an oven. Tubular blanks were lighter and stronger. The first rod makers to adopt the technology were a Californian collaboration between tournament caster Phil Clock, Dick Snyder and Don Green that founded the Fenwick brand. Their first generation patterns were cut from 'E-glass' cloths. The advent of 'S-glass' cloths offered a 30 per cent strength to weight ratio improvement over its predecessor. They contained more advanced low-alkali filaments, along with aluminium and manganese, and were bonded with phenol and polyester resins.

Fenwick again occupied the developmental high ground with the release of their HMG (high modulus graphite) fly rods—but were to lose the impetus that comes from being first when Don Green and Dick Snyder moved on to other ventures. A much respected identity, Don

A prince of a man, Don Green was a most influential identity in blank design and modern rod materials.

Australian saltwater fly original Max Garth fished through times when he adapted spin rod blanks and machined small saucepans for fly reel frames.

Green, established Grizzly, a name soon to be associated with quality fly rods. With Green at the helm that outfit went on to become Sage, the latter name coming from a suggestion from an advertising agency. Sage changed hands as Don Green went into retirement to spend his remaining years fishing. The sale saw in a change from a happy family atmosphere to hard corporate environment. Dick Snyder departed for the Australian beaches. In conjunction with Len Butterworth, a Brisbane based fibreglass rod maker, they set up B&S Laminates with mainstream production centred on surf fishing.

When machinist mate Gary Loomis discharged from the US Navy, valuable skills learned, he went to work for Dick Posey, steering Lamiglas on a steady as she goes course. Loomis was looking for a more adventurous ride and went on to set up Loomis Composites, a move that made it two big players in a one-horse town—Woodlawn, Washington State. From there it's a short hop to the Boeing works in Seattle. Some of the latest military jets are made there and have skins moulded from advanced graphite composites. American defence technologies that aren't too sensitive are handed over to the civilian sector. Being mates with famed aviator Chuck Yeager was a pivotal contact. Gary acquired the services of Steve Rajeff, who'd been winning spin, plug and fly events at world tournament casting championships since his teens. Sharing boats with Loomis, Yeager and Rajeff was stimulating and enriching…not that there was too much time for talking with a salmon run in full swing.

Following the company's sale, Loomis Composites morphed into Gloomis. Following the purchase of Gloomis by Shimano, American manufacturing operations were shut down and shifted to China. For a time the intensely competitive American rod market saw some big names locked in a modulus arms race. The times of Rick Pope sent a seismic shock through the rod making world. Motivated by what he saw as an upwards spiral in fly rod prices, the straight shooting Texan set himself the goal of making performance fly rods affordable. The flyfishing community responded by purchasing the Temple Fork Outfitters (TFO) brand in record numbers. Fly rod performance might be likened to gymnast scores at international level. There are a lot of 9.8s out there, some 9.9s and maybe the occasional ten. In an expansion into other arenas, TFO secured the services of Gary Loomis who went on to design an award winning series of spin and baitcast rods that represent remarkable value for money at US$99.95.

With Gary Loomis and Chuck Yeager on the Lewis River. Chuck with a nice salmon.

Them's the Breaks

For all the performance gains of graphite, there are tangible limitations. The higher the modulus, the lighter the rod—but the more unstable it becomes on deep bends.

Accidents waiting the happen lie in those seemingly innocuous knocks of everyday fishing, minor collisions between rod and any number of objects to be found around fisherfolk. Graphite is basically a brittle material and though many a post-knock inspection fails to reveal any damage, the foundations of a fatal rupture are there. Those micro-fractures inexorably grow like a stone chip on a windscreen. Given time, a progressive delamination occurs in the outer wall of the blank. Without the support of boding resin, further fibres fracture. Hot spots can remain until a decent fish comes along or can erupt under the impetus of a full-blooded cast. Interestingly, when a curve in a graphite rod reaches a critical mass, the implosion has its epicentre on the compression surface.

Bad knots and all, the overwhelming tensile strength of gel spuns has become a graphite graveyard for the careless. Back in days of mono and fibreglass, rod and line were more or less an even match and despite lots of

MORE ABOUT MODULUS

Modulus is a complex industry index. Basically, it relates to the resistance to bending of a single filament drawn from various alloys and extrusions. In rod making context, modulus is a measure of individual glass or graphite strands (per inch or centimetre) bonded within a cloth. The 'E' glass rods of the pre-graphite era had '30' modulus. Advanced graphite fibres used in the latest rod making cloths are in the 200 to 220 range. In the same context that various grades of steel or aluminium are offered to related industries, composites cloths are available in a range of industry designated moduli.

Rod makers—some, not all—have opted for standard references like IM6 and IM7, while others have come up with their own names. Names that the uninformed could construe as meaning some material discovery on the part of the rod maker rather than a catalogued cloths advance on the part of their supplier. Fly rods lead the way down this misinformation highway. The latest tech-sounding names to head up new rods relate to bonding resins—the mud and not the straw.

A modulus dead end awaits the arrival of new filaments. Metallic threads drawn from new super alloys are making their way into some cloths but comprise such a small proportion of the overall filament count that terms such as nano-titanium are a case of the tail wagging the dog. A breakthrough beyond graphite seems a matter of if rather than when. It would come as no surprise down the track to realise that like gel spuns, graphite technology remains a peak development.

THEM'S THE BREAKS

For all the performance gains of graphite, there are tangible limitations. The higher the modulus, the lighter the rod—but the more unstable it becomes on deep bends.

Accidents waiting the happen lie in those seemingly innocuous knocks of everyday fishing, minor collisions between rod and any number of objects to be found around fisherfolk. Graphite is basically a brittle material and though many a post-knock inspection fails to reveal any damage, the foundations of a fatal rupture are there. Those micro-fractures inexorably grow like a stone chip on a windscreen. Given time, a progressive delamination occurs in the outer wall of the blank. Without the support of boding resin, further fibres fracture. Hot spots can remain until a decent fish comes along or can erupt under the impetus of a full-blooded cast. Interestingly, when a curve in a graphite rod reaches a critical mass, the implosion has its epicentre on the compression surface.

Bad knots and all, the overwhelming tensile strength of gel spuns has become a graphite graveyard for the careless. Back in days of mono and fibreglass, rod and line were more or less an even match and despite lots of huff and puff, breakages under load weren't common. No so, gel spuns. Those in popular use on spin/plug tackle are more than capable of inflicting a fatal bend.

TAKING PRECAUTIONS

Whether fighting fish or trying to free snagged lures there are a few golden rules that will ward off accidental and unforeseen breakages.

- Apply pressure smoothly and never with a jerky motion.
- Avoid radical curves that take the blank beyond 90 degrees
- When attempting to free a lure that's stubbornly snagged, never apply pressure through the bent rod. Instead, point the rod at the snag.
- Never crank a fish closer than a rod length of line. At close range the upper part of the rod loses that cushion function so critical to netting or lipping operations. That close to a fish being unhooked it then becomes subject to all sorts of tortuous contortions.
- In staying clear of danger zones, fisherfolk will find themselves adopting lower rod angles. For anglers who habitually high stick and are stuck in their ways, life on the water may have to be an about face, a new leaf that'll save their fishing souls—along with some rods. Isn't that what seeing the light's all about?

huff and puff, breakages under load weren't common. No so, gel spuns. Those in popular use on spin/plug tackle are more than capable of inflicting a fatal bend.

As breakages of graphite rods reached proportions unheard of in the days of tubular fibreglass blanks, makers and marketers were forced into replacement policies that tended to absolve angler error rather than confront any lack of understanding of the curve parameter limitations of graphite rods and the overloading impact of gel spun lines in injudicious hands. Fishermen break more rods than do fish, and always will.

From guiding and travel perspectives there's a bit to be said about multi-piece rods. I frequently have folk aboard who're more tourists than anglers, and serial high-stickers—also major risks given fish sizes. It's easier to arrange a replacement section than be collecting another tomato stake. A replacement service, ten days from TFO's Texas facility to Australia, has got to be amongst the best in the business.

Major manufacturing shifts see rod making nowadays in the hands of folk who may have never seen a fish. American, Australian and Japanese rod companies have set up in China, Taiwan, Korea, Malaysia, Thailand and Vietnam. Labour costs and margins accommodate generous warranty arrangements.

Highs and Lows

Although not on the radar as HMG and GsP merged, the gutsier casting reels are a result of the union. This threesome creates a new performance plateau. Gel spuns have become an intermediary that redefines the roles of rod and reel.

In the past, the limitations of monofilaments have kept the playing field pretty level. To optimise casting efficiency and disguise presentations, thinking fisherman had little choice but to load reels with the lightest practicable lines.

The reserve power of gel spuns removes that burden and offers the flexibility of reversing some rod and reel functions. In essence, a rod can become less of a lever and a reel takes on an increased role as a winch. Within the realm of casting tackle, the design and function of rods on the spearhead now prioritises them as delivery vehicles—tools to enhance presentations, able to fight above their weight.

In place of the regimented up-down pump and wind, low rod angles flex the blank along its entire length.

American flyfishing greats Dan Blanton and Stu Apte discussing rod angles

Hand to hand with the River Rambo.

Black belt rodwork, you can be sure, it removes graphite blanks from that graveyard zone where expensive one piece rods turn into two useless pieces after being bent outside the envelope.

Low rod angles locate the bend down in the meatier butt section. In other words, the rod flexes through its entire length. This configuration generates pressures well beyond what the blank can deliver once the tip gets above waist height. The most energy efficient way to exert side pressure is to brace the butt under the short ribs and use body turn to generate a pump and wind on the horizontal plane. The technique works brilliantly well for getting the head of a strong fish in relatively shallow water. A fishing fact of life worth noting is that the higher the rod gets, the more the bend locates in the tip and the less pressure is on the fish.

Flatter rod angles transfer much of the load to line and reel. Modern baitcasters and spin reels are up to the job. Locomotive gears and Formula One drags smoothly deliver pressures once the province on light lever drag game reels.

Higher rod angles still have a role. But it's in the latter part of the fight, when the sting has been knocked out of the fish and line recovery is getting it closer to the boat.

The practised hand uses the limber part of the rod to cushion those lunges and headshakes that happen over the final stanza of a battle. This is where most fish are lost.

The flat stick fighting style dramatically shortens battles in shallow water. The technique is an adaptation of the 'down and dirty' fly rod fights pioneered in the Florida Keys. It's good to be able to release fish in good shape rather than at an exhausted stage. Catch and release has just been banned in Switzerland, thinking and responsible anglers worldwide are in the sights of those loonies.

Hookups that Hold

Fishing has been variously described as hours of daydreams punctuated by moments of panic. The latter period, that between hands-full to hands-on (the capture) can seem an abstract. Bouts seem much longer but most only last minutes. As for things to go wrong, there's a pattern. Most fish are lost through not being properly hooked in the first place. How many times do anglers cite being 'busted up' rather than admit tackle failure or flawed tactics? Saving the most painful till last, many a good fish gets lost at the boat through an injudicious act or omission. And fishing being so full of variables, luck and happenstance intervene at times both unwanted and fortuitous.

In times of fibreglass blanks and stretchy monofilaments, the slightest nibble may have deserved a shock and awe reaction. Those theatrics still happen but aren't really necessary anymore…not with a hi-modulus graphite rod strung with braid. Whether a curious tap or a full-blooded strike that nearly rips the outfit from your hands, the rod can be spared without ruining the hookup. The weight of the fish will become apparent as the line tightens and hooks take over. Sharp hooks. Fish don't have hands and tend to pin themselves.

A higher percentage of effective hookups happen with a simple one-two-three routine that takes less than a second…rod low, apply side strain and keep cranking… The way to max out a spin stick or trigger grip rod is to point it at the fish and (keeping rod and arms fixed in that position) turn the body 45 degrees. Body turn rather than elbow grease is a more efficient way to keep the heat on.

The next move depends on species and background. It should be an instant decision whether to get the head of the fish, or let it run and burn energy—in which case a higher tip lessens the strain on the hooks.

Hook holds always contain an element of risk that's beyond our control. More pressure increases the odds on coming unbuttoned, but not as much as jerky rodwork.

Dredging and shallower treatments

In accommodating waters deep and shallow, open or hazard strewn and fish that might be a thirty second affair or be capable of taking one beyond endurance levels, tactics need to be fluid with the situation.

A most effective deep water fighting technique on stubborn fish is to use the rod in the front lower

BANE AND ANTIDOTE

Attention to these details may spare some soul searching down the track.

Condition
Fish strikes but fails to hookup.

Causes
Blunt hooks.

Hooks too heavy in gauge to penetrate properly—a real sleeper.

Striking with the rod.

Moody fish not fully committed.

The 'X' factor.

Condition
Fish connects but hookup comes adrift at various stages and especially at the boat.

Causes
Hooks pull through too much drag pressure.

Tackle failure through lack of maintenance—worn line, fatigued knots, distorted split rings etc.

Failure to reduce pressure when fish under control and at close quarters.

Attempting to net green fish.

Lifting fish's head out of the water with rod.

Failure to create slack when fish leaps.

Prognosis
The security of hookups lies beyond the realm of science. Much depends on how fish take

and the extent of soft spots in and about the mouth region.

We've no control over where hooks anchor and the amount of firm tissue of the hold. However, one certainty is that compounding stresses as battles intensify and/or wear on, the odds on coming adrift shorten. This creates a couple of imperatives—use tackle that's up to task and get things over as soon as possible. Bear in mind however, that angler pressure should be a fluid dynamic. Skilled anglers are judicious in their applications but where possible, remain in charge.

Remedies
When retrieving point the rod tip at the lure.

Avoid any angle between the rod tip and the line. These will form where there's wind from a side-on aspect.

When using a twitch / rip / pause / crank retrieve cadence, keep slack line to a minimum. The rod rather than the reel works the lure. The major task performed by the reel is taking up the slack, however the amount left between pauses needs monitoring. Hookups on implosion feeders like bass, snook, tarpon and barramundi require some adjustment according to their mood. With the exception of largemouths, which have a relatively slow and gentle strike, hook sets can be more positive with the fish coming up tight onto the reel drag system rather than attempts through the rod.

FIGHTING FISH

Fighting Fish in Deep Water

By maintaining the hull in an upwind position fish will rise higher in the water column where more effective rod angles can be applied.

When the boat is downwind fish will dive deep and the fight becomes a slugfest. Boat handlers will find it necessary to re-position a number of times during a long fight.

For deep fights work the rod in a quadrant from the waterline to the gunwale.

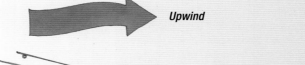

Upwind

Downwind

Fighting Fish in Shallow Water

Maintain the smallest possible angle between the line and the fish's tail. The most effective of all pressure angles is directly behind the fish in order to restrain forward motion. Again, boat handlers will find it necessary to re-position a number of times during a long fight.

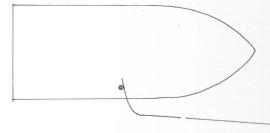

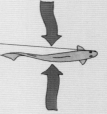

When fighting fish in shallow water, maintain the smallest possible angle between line and tail.

Rod Angles

The most energy efficient way to exert side pressure is to brace the butt under the short ribs and use body turn to generate a pump and wind on the horizontal plane. The technique works brilliantly well for getting the head of a strong fish in relatively shallow water.

quadrant—waterline to belt height. An abbreviated pump and wind within those parameters keeps the rod fully loaded. The lift provided by ocean swells can also be co-opted. By clamping the spool as the boat rises, fish are lifted a few more feet. Smart jigmen also synch the rise and fall of the boat to lift their jigs off deep reef and flutter them back down.

Billfish, big tuna and Volkswagen sized trevally are targeted by a gladiatorial breed of offshore angler locked and loaded with gel spuns. The direct contact afforded by minimal stretch and negligible influence of wind and wave can be used (along with a switched-on skipper) to shorten battles. By manoeuvring and maintaining the boat upwind of the fish, it will be encouraged to rise in the water column, whereby more effective rod angles and pressure can be exerted. If the boat is allowed to drift downwind, events turn into a slugfest, a fight for every inch. Big oceanic fish are adept at locating and lugging in a zone where angler pressure is least. It's important not to let them get too comfortable.

Low rod angles combined with body turn are a far more energy efficient and effective shallow water fighting technique than an up-down pump and wind with the rodwork in the vertical dimension.

The intensity of the resistance levels can be directly linked to pressure levels. California yellowtail, kingfish in Australia, and barramundi are classic examples. The harder the angler lays it on the more they pull. And visa-versa. The message is obvious—use a softly-softly approach in open water. The fish will tire. Amongst snags and jagged reef there's little option but to go for it right from the opening bell. Anglers on the receiving end of those jolting, king hit, close quarter strikes mightn't have any choice but a "stop 'em, or pop 'em" approach. But be ready to drop the rod and create slack when there's a leap. The move reduces the opportunity for gyrating fish to gain purchase against rod pressure and pretty much applies to all fish that leave the water.

Castles in Spain... in the shadow of... This angler maintains a high rod so's to keep his braided line clear of abrading rocks.

Sticks and Stones

Strong fish in heavy cover can go a number of ways. Some do half a lap around a stick, doubling back to effectively form a girth hitch in main line or leader. Mercifully, it can be over quickly.

Occasionally braided lines save the day by sawing through twigs. True braids are better suited than faster wearing thermofused GsP lines. There's a lot to be said in those situations for working the fish—if you can—high in the water column. If there's any place for redemption it's the thin end of trees.

Some fish miraculously manage not to hitch the line to an unrecoverable degree. Or bury an unoccupied hook in a branch, then wrenching themselves free. A surprising percentage will calmly swim out of trouble if given slack. The better anglers working the wood are deftly able, in a blink, to switch from attack to defence, going thumb lock to free spool, resuming the battle the instant there's direct contact again.

Boat handling figures in hand to hand fights. It's much more feasible to take the platform to the fish and attempt to undo things from there rather than trying to horse them back.

Over reef and amongst riprap, remember the kryptonite thing and lengthen leaders where necessary.

A spreading catch and release ethic has a cornerpost about getting the fight over and picture taken as soon as possible. This placed some priority on letting the fish go while it was still in good shape. The reserve power of GsP suits that end better than taking an already stretched mono to the limit.

Fights on Fly

Flyfishing is a special case, for two reasons. Gel spun backing allows anglers to stay in contact with big fish at distances never previously thought possible. These long-range links change the tactics and tempo of fights. Anglers have to battle for every inch, whereas an ideal situation is to recover backing and up the ante as the fly line comes back on the reel.

Of mountains of print on fly fishing, a Himalaya or so is devoted to preliminaries. What rods, reels and lines to use. How to rig it all, tie flies and cast. Far less ink is expended on what to do once the fly hits the water. And by the time we get to where a fish takes the fly, we're talking mere foothills.

A number of factors create that situation. Perhaps the most pertinent is that while there is no shortage of motivated anglers willing to attack a keyboard in the name of fly fishing, the majority fish for species that rarely, if ever, get into the backing.

It's easier to praise the casting performance of late generation rods and today's more aerodynamic lines than it is to write about redlining them on tough fish. You may read where it's possible to throw a fly further than a baitcaster and into places that cannot be attacked with treble armed lures. However, when it comes to yanking fish out, jaw dislocated and eyes crossed, we couldn't possibly be talking about fly rods. Could we?

The difference between fighting fish on conventional tackle and fly rods is a bit the same as comparing Marquis of Queensberry pugilism with kick boxing, kung fu, Liverpool street fighting and Tai chi, all rolled into one.

The flyrod offers a fighting flexibility whereby the line is retrieved by hand rather than recovered via the reel.

On conventional tackle anglers work the fish within range of net, gaff, or tag pole with a pump and wind routine. The cycle is standard and the no-no's—jerky rod work and high sticking, mainly—are few. Fights on run-of-the-mill tackle follow a fairly predictable pattern. Starting with a headlong rush the instant they're hooked, open water fish pour on the coals, leapers leap and bushwhackers head for snag heaven (or fly line hell, depending on what happens next). Then as encounters with the gallopers wear on, tiring fish unable to make headway will resort to hanging on one side low in the water. This loss of equilibrium signals an outcome that's just a matter of time.

The tactics one adopts in these fights are dictated by species, foliage and topography. There's a compelling case for proactive tactics when cover oriented fish are involved. In those hand-to-hand stoushes, fly line and leader become a veritable handline, when there's a hit the angler simply keeps stripping. The strip/strike is also the way to pin bones, poons, barra, billfish and a heap of others.

There's no set choreography on what to do the instant a strike happens. But lifting the rod is amongst the less efficient. Remember that the higher the rod, the more the bend locates in the tip, and the less pressure on the fish. Dry fly fishing for trout is an exception, but that's it! Trout are a kind of special case. The hooks on which flies are tied are sufficiently fine to be set with the minimal pressure that comes from lifting the rod. The pace of events tends not to be demanding of reflexes. With light tippets it is advisable to hold the rod tip high so that it cushions those lunges.

With snag dwellers and fish in 'softer' cover—assuming we're saddled with an adequate leader—a more effective extraction process is to point the rod at the fish and recover line as fast as you can. As the fish is prised out of its den, you should be able to reposition the rod sideways so that it becomes available as a shock absorber during that critical close range stage of the fight.

There's a compelling case for two fingers trapping the line on the rod hand instead of one. In close quarter's fights these override the reel drag, instantaneously applying stop and go pressures to the fly line. Anglers feeling their way through these fights in telephone boxes will probably experience the temptation to let the fish run for the sake of it getting it on the reel. Don't make that mistake.

Alternatively, when dealing with open water fish like tuna, flats trevally, mackerel and queenfish the idea is to let them run. The fly line has a drogue effect in the water. Built-in stretch combines with the limber fly rod to exert a jerk-free pressure that's more sleeping pill than electric shock, hooked fish are confused rather than alarmed. It's up to the angler. There will be surrounds where it is wiser to make the fish fight for every inch. But too much heat, too soon, too often results in tippets popping and hooks pulling.

The cumulative effect of not aggressively prosecuting the early stages of fights with hot runners is that by the time they get the message you've got a tired fish on your hands. Their energy levels are too depleted to do a real lot about the situation. Sneaky, yes, but that's the passive option on the fish—not all of them, mind you—that make long runs. Many a fight doesn't really start until the fly line begins coming back on the reel.

Open water 'hot runners' fall into a number of groupings, each calling for different tactics. Some, such as mackerel and billfish, should be allowed to make that furious first burst and follow-up runs with just enough drag on the reel to prevent an over-run as the backing is peeled. Others like trevally, kingfish and offshore bottom fish should be made fight for every metre. Your drag is on a hard setting before you start.

Flats situations are handled differently to battles offshore. The former sees the fish in sight for much of the encounter, thus allowing the angler to apply the most telling rod angles and pressures. In deep water, the fight turns into a more up and down affair. Boat positioning enters the dynamic. When the boat is positioned upwind, hooked fish often tend to position high in the water column. In the reverse situation it will lug deeper, making events much more of a time consuming grind for both angler and onlookers.

A significant tactical advantage stems from the knowledge that you're not going to run out of line. Peace of mind for one. The confidence factor can never be under-rated. Offshore flyrodding involves bigger boats, more folks aboard, and depends a lot on teamwork. When there's a hookup, having a big reserve of backing buys time to get the boat squared away before the rest of the blokes can join the fight. When it comes to taking on the strongest fish in the sea, its every tail beat drains away another dram or two of energy.

Bigger fish that run faster and further raise the issue of water pressure on regulation IGFA leaders. Thinner gel spun backing and shortened fly lines are compensatory measures. I've spoken to my mate Dean Butler about the impact of water pressure on tippets. If anyone would know, it's him. Dean has orchestrated a re-write of the IGFA world record marlin on fly chart. Water pressures, so far, haven't been an issue with 8 kg and 10 kg tippets. Middleweight billfish such as sailfish, white marlin and the juvenile black marlin along Australia's east coast are within the realm of 6 kg tippets. To rig lighter is to enter uncharted waters.

It's not unusual for hot fish to take hundreds of metres of backing. I've had close to a thousand out on a blue marlin better than 400 pounds. The bloody rod broke with the fish 'a spring creek cast away' after five hours. Dean Butler had a similar sized blue 700 metres out when it was sharked after seven hours. Three hours earlier, when Dean battled the fish alongside the boat, a crewman was catapulted into the water when he gaffed it. Had it been tagged, it certainly would have gone down

STAYING CONNECTED TO LEAPING FISH

White Belt Highsticker

When a fish leaps clear of the water or lunges through the surface, maintaining a high bent rod and a tight line direct to the fish isn't a good move. Fish leap as a means of divesting themselves of annoying objects, mostly something they're unable to swallow. Where it's a lure, either hard bodied or soft with weight (jigheads in particular) gyrating fish are assisted in gaining leverage and generating centrifugal force by pressure from the angler. Many fish are lost through this failing.

Black Belt Flat Sticker

By instantly dropping the rod and thrusting it forward, anglers create slack line, which in turn reduces the amount of torque a leaping fish can exert on the lure and body fittings.

Free-spooling Out of Trouble

Some fish do not deliberately head into snags with the same single minded purpose as those cover oriented, but given the amount of timber cover in many locations, snags getting into the act become inevitable.

A tactic that rescues many a dire situation is to put the reel in freespool when the fish takes the line

Take It to the Max

With a hard drag setting, maximum pressure from the rod is generated by having it flex along the entire length of the blank. This cannot be achieved with a rod tip that's above shoulder height; there the bend only locates in the top of the blank, its apex moving closer to the tip (with pressure on the fish actually reducing) as it gets pushed higher. The way to go when a max effort from the tackle is called for, is to keep the tip below belt height and use body turn to locate the fulcrum point on the bend as close to the reel as possible. This wrings a reserve power from the butt that lays dormant in the hands of highstickers.

around a snag, While using thumb pressure as a line control, re-position the boat to clear the line and re-engage the reel once there is a direct contact again.

Some anglers who've got things together have repeated the move a number of times during a battle in the sticks with a big fish.

as the biggest fish ever 'taken' on a fly rod. It certainly amounted to the most stirring bluewater battle I've witnessed.

Fights with big fish follow a sequence. The first thing is to ensure it is properly hooked and safely transferred to the reel.

When the run stops, and as follow up runs become shorter or change direction, the opportunity to start recovering backing will occur. Wherever possible do not fight fish on the backing. Recover line by cranking like hell, pump and wind is a waste of energy—yours—when working at long range. There's enough winch power in well made saltwater fly reels to keep the rod tip bent and to maintain contact.

If slack occurs—a change of direction on the part of the fish is a foremost cause—a fatal tip wrap can be one consequence when spooled with a gel spun backing. A preventative tactic is to thrust the tip into the water while continuing to crank flat-strap.

Fly rod battles with big fish are more physically taxing than other tackle. It's pretty much entry level to have the stamina to crank several hundred metres of backing onto a fly reel in a single burst, hard and even.

The next stage is to get as close as possible to the fish, generally a combination of boat manoeuvring and angler hard work. Fish resistance patterns intensify as they become aware of the presence of the boat. This is the signal to escalate pressure and calculate pressure angles.

No pressure direction saps fish energy reserves more rapidly than that coming straight over its tail to the head. This interrupts forward motion; fish with noted endurance must have a water flow over their gills. Anglers should be always striving to direct pressure from the rearward quadrants. This means sideways rod work

The higher rod angles employed in bluewater fights are dictated by fish that make very long runs, boat design and the deeper water.

and sudden repositions of pressure like the 'closing the circle' manoeuvre. The easiest way to implement these moves is always to be adjusting the direction of your pressure so that the angle between the leader and fish's tail remains as small as possible.

While most anglers are content with a healthy bend in the rod, it is not the way to wring maximum pressure from the blank. A flat-stick technique, also applicable to spin and plug tackle, involves locating the apex of the fighting curve as close as possible to the reel. With the rod locked in that configuration the angler pulls the fish towards him. Another way to visualise these red line loads is to think of the top two thirds of the rod flattened as more or less an extension of the line. The reel is at belt height, handles upward. Line recovery takes the form of short, rapid cranks, "keeping the fish's head" so to speak.

Flat sticking and closing the circle are tactics that come into their own when the fish is in sight. They can be sooner applied on flats fish than oceanic nomads like tuna and mako sharks. Unfortunately out on the offshore arena, high side rails can force anglers to compromise rod angles. Un-sharp skippers aren't much help, either. Both lengthen fights.

As the fly line comes into sight it's a good time to re-adjust the drag to a heavier setting. That move needs to be rehearsed until it can be done without diverting attention from fish. The dynamics of these battles on the high seas precludes the precise drag settings as applied to conventional tackle. Angler override enters the equation. Pinching the line is an advanced redline technique, you can be sure. Applied when using the rod to draw the fish closer, this rod hand thumb and forefinger 'clamp' prevents the drag from yielding. Seasoned bluewater flyrodders tend to trust their sense of feel more than the reel.

The arrival of the flyline back at the reel becomes a time when anglers need to be focused on breaking the resistance of the fish, wearing it down while there's still holding power in the leader. It's not unusual to recover a portion of the flyline only to lose it again. While this happens on a number of occasions on strong fish, there's light at the end of the tunnel as gains outdistance the losses. You're winning!

When a tail lobe breaks the surface, you've won. But don't go holding a victory celebration—not just yet. There's still a little bit of fishing left that requires your mind to stay in the job. The next fish lost through a lapse at the 99 per cent mark won't be the first.

The last decade has been especially exciting for big game fly fishing. The record charts have had their biggest shake up in years. Billfish records that many thought would never be eclipsed have been. The hundred pound tuna barrier has been smashed and tarpon marks have been pushed beyond two hundred pounds. It's fair to say that those captures mightn't have been possible back in days of Dacron backing.

THE BRUISE BROTHERS

The Seriola swim contains some major sportfish distributed through the temperate and sub-tropical coastal waters of the world's oceans. These bruise brothers are street fighters that travel in gangs through territories taking in reef, bottom rubble and wrecks. A deep bag of dirty tricks makes them short price contenders for the title of toughest fish in the sea.

The greater amberjack, Seriola dumereili, is the most widespread and quite possibly the largest. It ranges through the Atlantic, Pacific and Indian oceans. An all tackle record of 149 pounds still stands. As the name misleads, the Pacific yellowtail is a little more widespread. There are three sub-species, the California yellowtail, Seriola lalandi dorsalis, the southern yellowtail, Seriola lalandi lalandi (called the yellowtail kingfish in Australia and New Zealand where it reaches 100 pounds), and the Asian yellowtail, Seriola lalandi aureovitta. The fittingly named samson fish, Seriola hippos, seems an Australian species with a distribution along the lower half of the continent. It too, reaches 100 pounds.

Kingfish seem the most far ranging and will enter bays and harbours. It also hangs around any man made structure that attracts baitfish. This sometimes shallow habitat along with the beeline hooked fish make for underwater objects against which it rubs off lures, often breaking lines, compounds the difficulties in dealing with an already powerful fish.

The offshore amberjack and samson fish habitat—reef and wrecks from around 30 fathoms to the edge of the continental slope—is also likely to produce kingfish. Anglers fishing off Brisbane and similar latitudes off Australia's west coast have taken all three from the same water.

The braids era and accompanying cargo of gutsier reels and graphite composite rods that are lighter and stronger have opened up Seriola slugfests via deep water jig fisheries. Slim knife jigs with dazzling metallic finishes and fitted with loose assist hooks sink faster, deeper and are less taxing on elbow grease when it comes to their workings. A steady sink and draw that's synched with the rise of ocean swells can be just as effective as rip, tear and bust. Where tide and wind permit it may not be necessary to entirely retrieve jigs—a re-cycle to works the lower water column provides better exposure to fish that inhabit that zone.

Kingfish are curious and aggressive – habits that some optimistic anglers see as a death wish.

This Samson Fish came from the Southern Ocean off Kangaroo Island, South Australia

Chapter ELEVEN

IN CONCLUSION

The Sales Trail – Corporate Coalface to Consumer Cash

The pace of events at the corporate coalface has been anything but a slow boat to China. During the research and writing of the book, Chinese sources began offering line making companies raw GsP yarns they claimed as Dyneema. Tests proved otherwise, disclosing a polypropylene content. An inferior fibre.

Rather than leave the Chinese to their own devices, DSM has, at this writing, acquired a major shareholding in Shandong ICD High Performance Fibre Co Ltd, based in Laiwu, Shandong Province, China. This will have an impact on supply, and perhaps pricing.

Presumably, the status of DSM's Toyobo/Nippon Dyneema arrangements will remain unchanged, though word of what's happening in Japan seems to be as guarded as the attack plans for Pearl Harbour.

Previously, DSM announced special arrangements with the Pure Fishing empire, marketers of the Berkley, Fireline and Stren brands. The logical assumption there is one of cheaper raw material costs. The question for consumers is the ripple effect, if any, when anglers spool up.

Spectra has more than recovered any lost ground since manufacture transferred from Allied Signal to Honeywell Specialty Fibres. Backroom talk amongst makers of true braids is that Spectra handles better on their braiding machines.

Superline brands have gone from a trickle to a flood over the last few years. The vast majority are erected by marketing companies that do the packaging but out-source the making. The handful of makers that

actually market their own include Suffix plant in Taiwan, The Australian Monofil Company, and California based Western Filaments. In a move to counter the grip Sunline and Daiwa have on Japan's backyard network, Shimano have purchased Innovative Textiles, a big player on the stateside scene that makes the Power-Pro brand.

Some other significant tackle industry names have dealt themselves a hand in the braids business via contract arrangements with braiding companies. With inventories bolstered by braids, they are able to offer retailers attractive package deals offset by their mainstream rods, reels and hooks. It's not been unusual in back play for competing brands to come off the same assembly line. Lines can be chemically and physically identical, save for a different colour and packaging.

The braids marketplace is thus a spin doctor paradise. There are only so many ways of saying a line is thin, strong, wears, casts, lasts, handles and is round—but that hasn't prevented the hype from rising to political proportions. Extravagant claims about knot strengths are yet to be substantiated. Truth in advertising? The spin in support of low carrier braids rises in pitch. Hearts, minds and wallets are captured by buzzwords about braiding, bonding, body and revolutionary resins. Not the first time, by the way, that the mortar rather than the bricks sells a commodity. Despite the exhortations, gel spun polyethylene fibres remain resolutely impervious to chemical intrusion.

The media plays a major but shifting role. Seas of ink were initially splurged on the sensational feel from braids and positive / negative follow-ons. The tide went out till the next generation of gel spuns arrived. As the marketplace went into over-supply, generic references gave way to the battle of the brands. Fishing magazines can't exist without advertising revenue from the tackle industry. Thought many still have day jobs, writers with

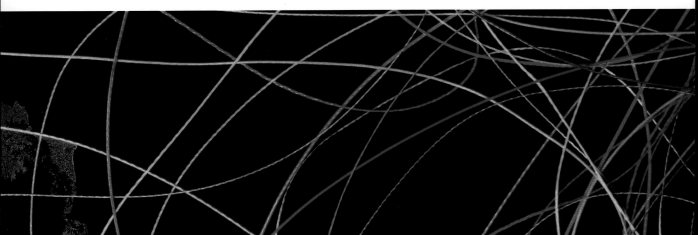

profile and by-line align with this company or that and receive support packages. Publishers and editors see to it that good advertisers also receive editorial support. Writers on the make need little encouragement. The greater scope television offers for product exposure has been seized on by producers. The programmes screened on Australian networks have degenerated into running commercials with talking head hosts force feeding product to the viewers who'll stay watching. The late Malcolm Douglas was a lone local exception, along with the wonderful fly fishing series, A River Somewhere.

Then there's the net. Fishing forums have opened a coalface where lines (and everything else used in fishing) can be proclaimed and condemned without the fair play and restraints of the mainstream media. Trial by media has become a big negative that tests the impartiality of moderators in these times when the net has conquered the tyranny of distance, reaching where fishing's print and electronic media may not. Anyone who can hit the water with a cast may have a say—a soapbox. Admirable though the democracy may be, issues too often boil down to exchanged views between the techno-savvy dude, who may or may not be able to fish, and worm-on-hook blokes who've never been further afield than the local creek. All things considered, the positives still outweigh the negatives.

Given the asking money for gel spuns, not everyone is able to try them all. Experienced anglers generally settle on a brand with which they're comfortable but still need to keep an eye on events. At a retail level, potential purchasers who're not sure of their exact needs can find themselves steered to a brand that contains the best retail margin. Tackle shop staff alike aren't immune from the braids' brainwashing that goes with a volatile marketplace. Much of the spin accompanying low carrier braids deals with bonding resins and the body they provide, albeit temporarily. Allowing for wonderful advances in alchemy, such talk is about the mortar and not the bricks. Gel spun polyethylene fibres remain impervious to chemical intrusion. All finishes are skin deep. It's an interesting exercise to toss around in a tackle shop terms like carrier, pik and denier. The looks say it all.

The day seems still a fair way off when there'll be truth in labelling. Where construction details of Spectra / Dyneema lines are displayed like nutritional values of the foodstuffs on supermarket shelves. Consumers spending that much money are entitled to know what they're really getting.

Braids have taken bluewater casting to the outer limits with popper crunching Volkswagen sized Giant Trevally.

Frequently Asked Questions

Are Spectra and Dyneema the same?

What is the difference between braids and gel spuns produced through other processes?

Why do some gel spuns cost more and others less?

What's carrier?

What's a pik count?

What's denier?

Why do I need a leader?

Is it possible for braids not to break at the knot?

Why do braids fade?

Does colour loss affect strength?

What is meant by the term body?

Which knots are best?

Will gel spuns work on all reels?

Do springy gel spuns cast better as some claim?

Do braids stretch?

What about claims that special resins make braids stronger?

Why do some braids cost more?

Where are braids made?

Why are there so many brands?

Do braids cut?

Do braids break rods?

Why are some braids sticky?

Is there a second generation gel spun fibre?

The badging of some braids carries additional letters that aren't explained. What do they mean?

Can gel spuns be used for baitfishing?

Do braids have good abrasion resistance?

What are the advantages for lure fishing?

Braids cost more than monofilaments, are they worth the money?

I'm thinking about trying soft plastics after having happily fished bait on mono for years, does this mean I also have to switch to braids?

Are Spectra and Dyneema the same?

Yes, same stuff. Everywhichway. The original raw yarn was called Dyneema by the people who developed the gel spun process. The rest of the world followed suit. But for reasons American, the name Spectra entered the lexicon after Netherlands inventors, DSM High Performance Fibers negotiated a manufacture agreement with those in the USA.

Allied Signal was an American company primarily involved with making body armour for the military and police. It decided on Spectra rather than adopting the existing Dyneema. Allied Signal developed the first designated gel spun fishing line, called Spiderwire. But when Allied Signal went about aggressively marketing in Europe, turf DSM considered theirs, DSM withheld technology and for a time, Spectra lagged.

The confusion has since diluted as anglers have become better informed. And while there has been some rearranging of the corporate deck chairs, DSM retains an overall interest. America is the world's largest producer of gel spun polyethylene. The Honeywell Corporation acquired Allied Signal and nowadays produces and exports Spectra and DSM produces Dyneema at a facility opened in North Carolina.

What is the difference between braids and gel spuns produced through other processes?

True braids are slower and more expensive to manufacture. They are produced at a snail's pace on banks of braiding machines that run 24/7. Fused gel spuns see the fibres bunched and passed through a heating element which melts the outside surface thus forming a coating.

Braids with high carrier and pik counts handle better and wear longer. Fused gel spuns are a cost effective choice in single digit breaking strain but take on an increasingly wiry texture as diameters increase. With hard use, the wear rate of fused lines requires monitoring. A fuzziness is an accelerating consequence as the outer surface chips and flakes to expose fibres.

Why do some gel spuns cost more and others less?

Retail costs are, or at least they should be, a reflection of the costs of the raw yarn that goes into their construction and the manufacturing process. Fused and coated lines are less costly to make than true braids. High carrier braids costs more to make than those constructed of fewer strands of raw GsP yarn. The finer the denier of the raw yarn the more it costs.

DSM currently produces Dyneema in descending deniers SK60, SK65 and SK75. A price difference ascends by 50 per cent between types. A similar situation applies with Honeywell which produces Spectra 1000, Spectra 2000 and a finer denier that will probably have the designation of Spectra 2200. A similar range produced by Nippon Dyneema is said to include deniers that are finer still—but not exported.

What's carrier?

Carrier is an industry term that defines the number of strands of a specific denier that are used of in the construction of braided lines. The raw yarn is supplied in bulk spools that are mounted on braiding machines according to the specifications of the line to be produced. Braiding machines can take up to 12 spools, however a 12 carrier braid becomes cost prohibitive while not delivering the same percentage quantum increase in performance and durability that an eight carrier braid delivers over a four strand construction.

What's a pik count?

Pik is another braider term used to define the tightness of the weave. When applied to braids, the pik count is based on the number of times per centimetre an individual strand meets an imaginary straight line along the outer surface of the line that's parallel to the core. Eight is the magic number for braids. Lower pik rates produce lacy lines with unsatisfactory handling, higher pik lines are prone to fatigue problems due to the very brittle nature of GsP fibres.

What's denier?

Denier is yet another index. It is used as a measure of the microscopic diameters of various fibres.

Why do I need a leader?

Leaders weren't on the menu when Spiderwire was first released. Those early users, mostly American bassmen, went bareback. For those concerned about the visibility factor of a line having a solid colour, big retailers like Bass Pro and Cabelas began to sell brown and green marking pens to camouflage the working end of the line. They saw limited use. When braids reached Australia, leaders were already entrenched and automatically became part of braid rigs. Moreso, in fact, given tough fish and terrain that are hard on lines.

Leaders perform a number of essential tasks. In finesse fishing they disguise the presentation, hence the popularity, real or imagined, of fluorocarbons. At the heavy duty end of the spectrum there's the teeth, raspy jaws and razor sharp gill covers of popular fish like barramundi, tarpon and the mackerel family. Rock, reef and snaggy situations introduce more hazards into the equation that can require more length in a leader. Offshore anglers tend to use stout leaders extending from a rod length to the allowable 9 metre lengths under IGFA rules. Bluewater tasks range from deep jigging, billfish trolling, deep sea baitfishing, and casting chuggers / stick baits around remote reef.

Is it possible for braids not to break at the knot?

Yes, if there's a defect somewhere in the line. A manufacturing glitch may be at fault but these are very rare occurrences. The broken fibres that go with hard fishing in tough terrain is a far more common culprit. Otherwise, and on any intact line, knots are the weak point and the seat of any rupture. That goes for every known knot and those yet to be devised.

Why do braids fade?

GsP fibres are impervious to chemical intrusion. The various pigments that makers give their lines are skin deep and will fade with wear. This can take years. Colour loss has become less tangible as improved resins and bonding technologies have become available.

Does colour loss affect strength?

There is no connection between fade and any loss of tensile strength. There are case histories of braids eventually fading to the off-white of the raw yarn but still going strong after a decade or more of yeoman service.

What is meant by the term body?

Consumers regularly come across this one on packaging and advertising blurbs. It implies a round format that retains shape rather than flattens. The presence of body in a braid results in reduced handling hassles, and visa-versa. Body in a braid is more a consequence of carrier and pik counts rather than the result of resins. Resins and additives are enhancements that eventually leech from the line. Gel spuns produced through fusing and coating technologies become malleable with use and noticeably flatten.

Under magnification, a four carrier braid has a squarish cross-section, while a five carrier is more hexagonal. The octagonal format of an eight carrier braid is as near as possible as technology can come to producing a round braid that retains body throughout the spool life of the line.

Which knots are best?

There is no such thing as a 100 per cent knot. Not in gel spuns, whether braided, twisted or fused. Any knot that delivers 70 per cent is a good outcome, but unlike monofilaments where a bad knot isn't hard to spot, in gel spuns you'd never know. Some knots that look the goods barely break at 50 per cent. For that reason the stated breaking strains on the packaging of many brands reflect unknotted tensile strengths upwards of twice those achievable with the best rigging.

Braid attached to leader material using a Slim Beauty Knot.

Things tend to even out and for most intents and purposes, what's stated on the spool is, more or less, the poundage actually being fished. As far as individual knots are concerned, the palomar knot delivers the most consistent percentages when gel spuns are attached to terminal tackle with a jam knot, moreso when tied with the gel spun doubled or trebled. For gel spun to leader connections, the Harro knot (christened by others) evolved from the Albright after bouts with the slim beauty.

Will gel spuns work on all reels?

Indeed they do. Types I can vouch for include spin, baitcast, and fly reels. I've a light braid on a sidecast outfit I use for freshwater and inshore baitfishing and a heavy braid on a bigger sidecast/centre pin that's the best choice for deep sea bottom fishing. My bluewater jigging threadlines are loaded with braid along with a lever drag gamefish reel. Catching billfish on braids is an entirely different sensation to using mono.

Reel makers have responded to the gel spun age with vastly improved line laying mechanisms that provide an even spread.

Do springy gel spuns cast better as some claim?

Absolutely not. The notion that springy lines aid casting efficiency got started back in mono days and has been with us ever since. All things considered, springy lines will disadvantage a caster, moreso those spooled with gel spuns. Any inherent tendency to lift off the spool, whether fixed or revolving, sews the seeds of a snarl.

Do braids stretch?

Some do. The raw GsP fibres contain 3.5 per cent stretch. While this figure remains a constant, the concertina affect of an eight carrier / eight pick weave builds up to an 8 per cent stretch factor into the line.

What about claims that special resins make braids stronger?

Not so! The tensile strength of Spectra / Dyneema lines is the sum total of fibres used in their construction, nothing more. The various eurethane based chemicals used to seal the fibres—albeit temporarily, allowing for the ten year spool life of some lines—do enhance handling and buffer knots against jerky applications of pressure. Claims to the contrary talk up the mortar while saying nothing about the bricks.

Why do some braids cost more?

The biggest margin along the maker / marketer / vendor chain goes to the retailer.

Market forces should determine what consumers eventually pay but that can be offset by pro-active marketing that includes 'in your face' tele-fishing.

At a manufacturer level, a scale of costs is directly related to the amount of raw yarn used in the process, the process itself—whether braiding or otherwise, and if the former, the carrier and pik counts. At retail level, fused gel spuns should cost less.

Anglers have the choice of a lesser outlay than for braids but a shorter working life.

Where are braids made?

Gel spun lines are produced in North America, Europe, Japan, Taiwan and Australia. It seems inevitable that China will expand in line making but as to the quality, who knows? A reputation as a bad world corporate citizen, China is already hawking an inferior and unlicensed so-called gel spun polyethylene yarn to braiders in other parts of the world. Analysis suggests it contains a high percentage of polypropylene, which has vastly inferior tensile strength. DSM has litigated against patent infringements but whether Chinese copycats will be (or can be) contained remains an open question. One reality though, the quick quid generally prevails over quality.

Why are there so many brands?

The growth from just a handful of brands to a situation where there are more than can be named reflects dynamics that go beyond straightforward demand and supply. There are many more brands than there are makers. These are manufactured on a contract basis by companies that may also produce their own brand. Some competing brands come from the same plant and have an identical construction but for colour and a different slant to wording on the packaging. The majority of current brands have been erected by marketing companies. A trend amongst big players in the tackle industry is to offer retailers gel spuns badged with their flagship brand. Those situations offer retailers the pricing flexibility that goes with having rods, reels and other tackle as part of the one deal.

Do braids cut?

Gel spun lines under load are capable of grooving and cutting various smooth surfaces, though not to the degree cited by some hearsay. Braids have been blamed for grooving rod guides. Although that could be the case of poor quality guides, I'm yet to see any damage from the passage of gel spuns, under tension and otherwise, being caused to reputable guide brands. Careless fingers are always a risk when gel spuns are paying out under pressure. Gel spuns exhibit exceptional abrasion resistance when in contact with smooth surfaces such as inundated and sunken timber. A capacity to saw through aquatic vegetation is a godsend when on a good fish.

Do braids break rods?

Braids do not break rods, anglers do. A majority of breakages occur when inexperienced anglers become snagged and attempt to free the lure by applying pressure through the bent rod. Breakages of this nature reached epidemic proportions as the number of converts to gel spuns climbed. This forced quality rod makers with big market shares into replacement policies that verge on an incentive to break rods.

Less common, but still significant are breakages that happen while fighting fish. Some are due to the sheer pressure overload that braids permit anglers to (unwisely) apply. Some inexplicable breakages happen where the blank may, unbeknownst to the user, have taken a knock in the past. It's unfortunate when the bend from a good fish becomes the final straw.

Very occasionally, sustained stress at a lockup point will cause a blank to de-laminate and rupture. It happened to me one time when flyfishing for marlin with Jack Erskine. I'd a blue well over 400 pounds and was into the 5th hour of a fight on a #15 weight outfit and 10 kg regulation IGFA tippet. With the flyline more than halfway back on the reel and the marlin looking pretty much at a standstill, high in the water column at the back of the boat, the butt section of the three piece fly rod suddenly snapped.

Why are some braids sticky?

There is a cheap and nasty class of braid that is made by a twist and wax process. Those I've seen are a green colour and come from the same European source though bearing different labels. Their main identifying feature is a sticky, waxy surface that impedes casting. Things get worse as the wax finish rapidly leeches from the working line. Handling hassles increase as the exposed fibres undergo accelerated wear and tear.

Is there a second generation gel spun fibre?

At this writing, not that I'm aware. Whether Dyneema or Spectra, variations are confined to deniers. But as finer gauges have become available, this has been seized upon by marketers who've stretched reality with claims that this represents a second generation. DSM has announced, amid some ado, a close collaboration with Pure Fishing, formerly Berkley and a former Spectra consumer. Whether this is a move to consolidate now that Honeywell is full steam ahead with Spectra, or a sign of things to come, remains to be seen. The acquisition of multiple brands by Pure Fishing makes them the biggest name in the tackle industry, lines included.

The danger zone...bends beyond 90 degrees in graphite rods and reels spooled with braid. It's not widely known that when a rod breaks through a severe load and an imprudent angle, the seat of the rupture happens at the compression surface.

The badging of some braids carries additional letters that aren't explained. What do they mean?
Those letters are acronyms thought up by marketing people. They deal in superlatives, sound impressive and obviously sell product. Does this mean a better braid, than, say, some under sung brands? Not necessarily.

Can gel spuns be used for baitfishing?
Absolutely! Braids have been a deep sea godsend. The uptake hasn't been as far reaching with bread and butter estuary anglers though there is much to gain. Specialised situations such as float fishing for luderick and fishing bubble floats and bait for trout have been the evolution of 'hollow' braids that float. Situations where the wisdom can be questioned include fishing from rock platforms and breakwalls.

Do braids have good abrasion resistance?
Were gel spuns the diameter of monofilaments in common use they'd be bulletproof. Within dynamics to do with abrasion resistance, diameter is the foremost factor in determining how well a line wears and for how long. Conversely, lack of diameter is a big virtue with braids. All things considered, the stuff vastly outlasts any monofilaments of equivalent cross-section.

In a nutshell, braids retain excellent togetherness and resilience in contacts with smooth surfaces—seasoned snags, aquatic vegetation and the like. The danger zones are sharp, raspy surfaces such as rock, riprap, reef, mangroves and other estuarine barnacle and oyster encrusted objects and structures. A single touch under load can be the kiss of death.

What are the advantages for lure fishing?
User benefits for lure fishers are a double-edged sword. Every user takes advantage of the passive feel and situation awareness braids deliver. As experience levels increase, a proactive edge, never possible with monofilaments becomes apparent—or should. Anglers are able to add retrieve inflections like never before. Mono or braid, it's not so much the lure, but what the users do with them.

Braids cost more than monofilaments, are they worth the money?
Amongst those still not convinced, purchase decisions can be penny wise but pound foolish. The simplest way I can put things is to cite the cost differentials between a quality copolymer and a braid having a good reputation. Going rates are heavily weighted, braids can cost up to four times as much. Do they outlast monofilaments by that ratio? Betcha! And then some... lots more!

I'm thinking about trying soft plastics after having happily fished bait on mono for years, does this mean I also have to switch to braids?
If you're serious, yes. Soft plastics are all about feel and touch. Soft plastics pioneers like Wayne 'Buff' Ross and

Kev 'Capt'n' Gleed, along with others were fluent back in mono days but were still left feeling the way like a blind man on a honeymoon. Contacts become much more defined with braids. Whether weed, rock, sand, mud or snag there's no more guesswork. Nor a lot of striking on suspicion. Whereas mono dilutes the message that a fish is there, by comparison braids amplify the message.

Last Cast

It's funny the way time mutes what once was, and what now is. Before attacking this last block of text—in a mood, I guess, akin to a horse that's sniffed the home paddock and just in case I'd missed something, I re-spooled one of my workhorse reels with mono and launched the boat.

It was a time-warp experience. I couldn't cast as far and the feel at the reel reminded me of wrestling with the steering wheel of my dad's De Soto when I first learned to drive.

Déjà vu, de-sensitised... and then some.

It turned out to be a short spin down memory lane. The barra weren't all that willing and, though I was, retarding reflexes to get in synch with the tackle was too big a step back into the past. The notion occurred that braid on a broom handle might well deliver more feel than mono on the latest Loomis.

Nope, there'll be no going back on what's gone down in this book. Nor, end of story, to monofilament mainlines. In that conclusion, I'm not alone.

My mono daze included this Dorado taken in the Parana River, Paraguay.